Yvonne Carol is the "nurse's nurse." A nurse treats the body, but Yvonne shares experiences of witnessing forces beyond our normal understanding. A nurse deals with the physical body and other forces like emotional energy and mental images or even psychic events. To be present at the time of "seeing" this "stuff" brings a realization that we live in a world that we are discovering is miraculous.

—Jay Harris, B.A., B.Div., M.S. Div, author, musician, artist.

Daily Miracles and Encounters of the Other Kind

Through the eyes
of a Visiting Nurse

Yvonne Carol Palese, RN, BS., CYT

DAILY MIRACLES AND ENCOUNTERS OF THE OTHER KIND

Copyright © 2023 Yvonne Carol Palese

Paperback ISBN: 979-8-238339-1

All rights reserved. No part of this publication may be reproduced or transmitted in any form or by any means, electronic, mechanical, photocopying, recording or otherwise, without written ermission of the publisher. Published by Yvonne Palese, contact at ycpalese@aol.com

Cover art by Yvonne Carol.

All names changed to protect their privacy.

Printed in the United States of America.

To my dear and very patient husband, Anthony F. Palese; my precious daughters, Trina Grogan and Nicholena Richards; and my beyond tolerant sons-in-law, JD Grogan and Darren Richards. This dedication also includes many friends and family that put up with my constant tales (which continue to this day), listening to me excitedly tell my many strange tales throughout the years.

In gratitude, Yvonne Carol Palese.

Contents

1. My Near-Death Experience 11
2. Guide from Being Lost 14
3. Ninety-year-old on Hospice 15
4. Joyful Mr. G. 17
5. Young Man too Young to Die 20
6. Twenty-year-old with Gunshot Wound to the Head 23
7. My Purse Lost in the Snow 26
8. Killer on His Chest Tattoo 29
9. Gunshot from Gang 33
10. 35,000 Feet Up 36
11. Twin Babies 43
12. The Diplomats from India 45
13. Gang Member Quadriplegic 49
14. Allie, too Young to Die 52
15. Man at the Gym 56
16. Magical Peacocks in My Yard 59
17. Dangerous Blue Eyes 64
18. On My Watch in CCU, Man Awakens 67
19. 400-pound Patient Won't Get out of Bed 70
20. No Autism for This Little Two-year-old Boy 75
21. Woman and Little Invisible Child 79
22. Life Without Her Leg 82
23. Sharks Below 85
24. A Six-month Contract Checking on Disabled Children 89
25. The Blue Nail Polish Opens His Eyes 92
26. A Dream of an Old Friend from High School 96

27. You Need to Find God...99
28. Mother's Death 104
29. ET Murphy from Above 108
30. "Am I a Man or a Woman?" 113
31. "I Will Come Visit You When I Die." 116
32. Oppressive Black Burkas 119
33. Car Repair - A Sign!...123
34. Homeless Man on the Street - A Message.............125
35. First AIDS Patient in 1982 127
36. Darkness..132
37. Living Next to Darkness..137
38. Scared to Death 143
39. Sex, Anyone?...147
40. A Soul Connection..149
41. Sick Doggie 153
42. My Hindu Patient..155
43. Giving Away Her Heart...158
44. Is Anyone Listening?...162

Introduction

Back when I was in my twenties, my life used to be a day of having lunch and shopping at Saks 5th Ave! But then my life changed when I had a spiritual experience, a personal experience, an inner calling to live my life in a new way. This happened at a time when I was reading Revelation in the Bible and had an awakening with the Living Christ. So, my life became one of purpose and a journey of self-discovery and inner knowledge through life and its lessons. I left the life I had known and blindly on faith stepped into undiscovered territory and eventually became a visiting nurse.

The journey took me to nursing school (I had been an art major.) Right from nursing school I became an ICU/CCU nurse. I worked in the hospital for five years and had many extraordinary experiences with illness, death, and dying, and seeing the horrific and the miraculous!

The following stories are true personal experiences as I encountered and witnessed supra-natural forces that are always working around us, whether we are aware or not.

Being a person of faith but also interested in the arts and science, these encounters and witnessed happenings were always viewed as gifts given to me and really seeing higher life forces around me. Every experience has only enhanced my life to an overall larger picture of the world than I originally had seen.

These happenings span over forty years of collected data that I have been writing down and keeping with the hope of sharing with others one day. Today is the day!

1

The Mysterious Miracle

My Near-Death Experience

Before I had my epiphany and found a real beginning to my purpose in life and towards my nursing career, the following happen during my searching. There was no question I had some real revelations and personal spiritual encounters but still did not have my direction clear yet. My focus and attention were on my husband and small child. During this time while still in my twenties, I was having many health issues primarily female, which I now know was part of how I was living and thinking, and my emotional state of wanting another child. I had so much more growing to do myself. We had no health insurance so that, too, was stressful!

I developed a large cyst in my right ovary, which was very painful. I went to different doctors for opinions. Boy, what an eye opener to the medical world that was for me. One doctor wanted me to have a complete hysterectomy without examining me! Another said remove the ovary. Others said it's all in your head. I was so shocked, but something in me knew something was very wrong. My inner voice was getting weaker and weaker listening to the professionals.

A year went by and then one day I called a doctor friend of mine and told him I was going to put a gun to my head! He was a lung specialist, but he said, "Wait. I'll call my good friend who is a top OB/GYN and see if he will take your case." I think I scared him. When he called back, he'd managed to get me an appointment for that afternoon. During my appointment, I finally felt I was in the hands of a very caring special man and doctor. He explained to me that he wanted to try a new surgical procedure that had not been done in the United States only in England. He was studying out of a manual and would like to try it on me and three other young women in about one week. I agreed.

The day of my surgery my doctor friend came into my room and explained I would be the third case to go into surgery because he was nervous that it had never been performed before and that two other women would go before me. I felt like he was my guardian angel looking after me. This procedure was going to be the first laparoscopy done in the US! Today, it is a very well-known surgery used all over the world.

Now the reason this story is so important is the fact that I almost did not make it after the surgery! I had a near death experience. At the end of the surgery, even though I was completely sedated, I could hear the nurses and doctors in a panic. They were unable to get any vital signs from me. I had a complete sense of my true self like another being living inside this body that had given me so many problems. This was the first time in a long time I was at rest, free of pain and really liked the feeling of not being tormented by this body! I was very aware of the nurses and doctors running around me in a panic saying,

"I can't get any vital signs here, call Dr. so and so!" When I heard this, I thought to myself, Oh what is everyone so shook up about? I am fine right here and at peace. I can come back and get my vital signs back when I choose to come back. Then suddenly I felt a shock in my body and I was somewhat awakened! There were about four to five nurses and doctors around me, rubbing my hands and feet. The nurse commented, "We have vital signs, Dr." To tell you the truth I was not happy at that point! I loved the quiet stillness I experienced with awareness and mindfulness, but the body was out!

During this time before awakening, I heard all that was going on in the room but like from a distance. I was in darkness and never left the body, but it seemed I had a choice to come back if I wanted but instead was shocked into coming back. During the time in the darkness, I felt OK there for a while. Like having a rest from pain and earthly things.

I saw no white light nor had communication with any being higher than myself. And that is the scary part of the experience. I realized later at home I had almost died, and I had not encountered anything of a higher nature! The reality hit me that I have not been living my life to the fullest and not accomplishing all I needed to accomplish while on planet earth! This was my first awakening to get to work and seek the Higher and the Divine's will for me. This is when I was led to enter nursing school and began my service that changed my life and took me into areas of life and the lives of others of the unknown for over forty years.

2

The Mysterious

GUIDE FROM BEING LOST

While driving eighty miles to an unknown area outside of Los Angeles to see a patient (no GPS at that time), I became lost in a dangerous industrial area with very few people around. As I pulled over, scared, lost, and trying to get my bearing set, I looked out the window and no one was near me. In fear, I dropped my head and tried to collect myself. I started to ask for help and directions. Feeling my body shaking, I could not look up! Then someone out of nowhere started to tapping on my window!

"Why are you here, Yvonne? You are in the wrong area; you need to get out!"

I slowly lifted my eyes, and my eyes met his. Trying not to be a victim or just seeing myself wanting to be saved, I had a sense of trust, but I would not roll down my window. As my eyes investigated his, he told me very loudly what I had done wrong. "You turned left instead of right, and you are not safe in this part of town." As he instructed me very nervously, he pointed and gave very direct instructions as to where to go. Help seemed to drop out of nowhere and I was back on my way in the right direction.

3

The Mysterious
Ninety-year-old on Hospice

I arrived to visit a patient in his late nineties to evaluate if he was to go into hospice care. His wife informed me that she was his caregiver. She was probably in her late eighties, bright, gracious, and an inspiration! A little Pomeranian puppy ran about under our feet in a joyful, playful manner as we walked to the bedroom. In the room in a hospital bed lay her husband in a semiconscious state.

Going about my nursing business, I began to ask her questions about his condition and about him. She said, "Oh, he is the dear of my life! We both met after our first spouses died. He was eighty, I was seventy. My friend introduced us, but it was all by telephone. He lived 135 miles away but after a few phone calls we were taken by each other so he would drive those miles every week for a year until one day he said, 'This is killing me to drive this far, want to get married?' Of course, I agreed at that point. We have had a wonderful life and very blessed!"

I mentioned I did not see how she could take care of him.

"Oh, I don't mind; he is the love of my life and I am a woman of faith. After we got married, we joined our families and had a huge lovely yellow farmhouse where everyone would come visit for the holidays. I was welcomed and loved by his family. You will meet his son later; he is coming to help in a few days."

I came back to visit for a final nursing visit before he was to be transferred to hospice. Again, his wife met me and invited me in. This time, though gracious, I could sense a sadness in her. She informed me that when her husband's seventy-year-old son had arrived to help her with his father, he had slipped in the shower and was hospitalized. They did not expect him to live! This woman was still like a rock and compassionate!

One week after this visit, hospice informed me her husband had died and her son. On Saturday, the families would gather from all over the country and there would be a double funeral for their father and son. This being a final celebration of life but gone together!

4

The Miracle
JOYFUL MR. G.

One night while I was working at the hospital, things were just calming down. All my patients had received their dinner and were cleaned up and ready for bed. I had just sat down at the nurse's station to complete my evening charting. It was a time to breathe and take a quiet moment.

The hospital was constructed in a circular floor plan with the nurse's station in the center and a small desk outside patients' rooms every so many feet so you could have the chart, write, turn, and almost have a 180-degree view into patients' rooms. It was the same on the other side as well.

It was probably close to ten o' clock and my shift would go until eleven. As I started to chart, I heard a very vivacious man talking on the other side of the nurse's station. His voice was so captivating it was difficult to finish my work. I decided I should hurry and go around the corner to meet him and see what he was so excited about and what his story was. It was not that he was speaking loudly but rather in a quiet, very exuberant manner. He was mindful that others were trying to go to sleep for the night. As I turned the corner, standing there in his hospital gown (open in the back with him holding onto it) he seemed so happy while talking to his nurse. I wanted to hear his story and be a part of all this joy! Mr. G. was sharing a story from his life and what had happened to him.

In his early forties (he was now about eighty), he had just gotten married and purchased a new car.

He was in his new car and was in a horrid car accident that left him holding onto life, He was taken to the hospital where the staff worked on him. They saved his life but he remained in a coma.

"I was basically alive living in a black hole for over six months." He said he could hear all that was going on but could not respond in anyway. He heard the doctors and nurses talk as if he was dead and not present.

They performed the daily routine of washing him, giving him medicine, IVs, and keeping him alive with a tube feeding. His young wife stopped coming and eventually divorced him. He said he was being tortured emotionally but had no pain or discomfort in his body.

At first, he tried in vain to talk to the nurses and others but could not reach them. "Hey, I am here! Can't you hear me?" All to no avail! He proclaimed he felt like his full self on the inside, but the outer body was almost dead to the world. After a time, he stopped trying to reach out to the outer world and accepted this black hole he was now condemned to.

The real internal struggle continued until he realized he was only fighting himself and his situation was probably just hopeless. He was experiencing living hell. After several months of this darkness, he finally relented and started calling out internally to God if he really existed. This went on for a short while until he said he was a broken spirit. Then suddenly there was a real encounter with the Almighty God consciousness! He began a daily walk, prayer, and personal relation with the Lord. He tried to bargain and beg for forgiveness for all wrongdoing and the path his ego had taken. He asked for a new chance to be healed and if He did that for him, he would never stop proclaiming His Glory on earth! So that is exactly what he has continued to do, and I then got to witness and also hear the joy and proclamation of healing promises!

5

Unknown/Compassion

YOUNG MAN TOO YOUNG TO DIE

As a young nurse, I had just arrived at the hospital for my 3–11 p.m. shift in the medical surgical unit. I always liked the pace of this shift because it was a quieter, calmer time of the day in the life of the hospital environment. Walking down the hall, checking on my patients, I came to the room of one of my patients whom I knew was a young man in his thirties with terminal lung cancer. At his side was a beautiful young woman whom I found out was his life partner (they were not married). She stood draped over him, crying, her beautiful chestnut brown hair covering his chest as she tried to embrace him. Sorrow filled the room, bringing a feeling of heaviness and adding to the air a sense of tightness. I had to be self-aware and breathe myself to be present. My attention had to be focused on me to be aware and open to all that was going on and to bear the pain taking place in the room. Grounding my feet into the floor and connecting with my breath helped along while saying an internal prayer!

As I cautiously approached the bed to check my patient, his girlfriend slowly looked up at me, meeting me eye to eye. Mindfully, I checked on him, explaining to both what I needed to do in addition to checking his vital signs. It was obvious this patient was failing and would not be here very long. Once finished, I sadly left the room to return to my other patients. What was fascinating was my sorrow was not so much for the young man but from the pain and messages resonating from the young woman! It was very intense and almost unbearable. But I had to continue because I had five other patients that needed my attention. As I worked my shift her pain and presence were with me.

After several hours of work, I took a break and went down to the café, which was not usual for me. There, sitting alone in the corner, was this beautiful girlfriend of my patient. I was drawn to her and asked if she would like company. She agreed, but I was cognizant that she hesitated. As I sat beside her, she looked into my eyes and started to cry. The tears were uncontrollable as she shared her life's story with me. She told me how much in love she was with him and that they lived their dream in the country for several years. They had hoped to have children one day, but now their family was with the dogs. That was a joy for them. His family had never accepted her and now, with no marriage and him sick, the entire family had taken over all decisions and because of not legally being married, she had no rights. She was totally alone, pushed and treated as an outsider! Her own family, which was few, lived a great distance away. This was in the 1980s so there were no cell phones for communication. I, a stranger, was there for her! Open to the call of caring and stepping into her pain, I could see the gifts and the love being received and given by two humans. She told me I gave her the courage to move forward and face all that was before her. This was all through caring and listening to her story. To simply be present in myself and to have a real exchange with another human being. This is the gift and joy of life and sharing of ourselves no matter what your faith is or how you believe. Extending compassion, a listening ear, and love!

6

Darkness Farthest from the Light

Twenty-Year-Old with Gunshot Wound to the Head

As a young nurse I went to work in a hospital. What a shock this was to my eyes. I loved caring for the patients and the excitement of the hospital environment, but some of the encounters were unbelievable!

This story is one of them.

As I received my patient load, I was informed I would have a lighter case load due to one problem patient who would need my extra time. His name was J., twenty-eight years old, in the hospital from the aftermath of a gunshot to the head after a drug deal went bad. He had limited understanding of his situation and was a very angry young man. That would be well understood for anyone to go through such a horrid situation. He had been placed in a private large room at the end of the hall so as not to disturb other patients. Entering the room, I saw a nice-looking young man peering at me, his white sheets pulled up to his eyes.

All his external wounds were healed, but you could see in his eyes that he was scared and fearful. Full of compassion, I tried to comfort him, explaining what I was going to do along with taking his vital signs. His eyes softened and he allowed me to do the task. Having somewhat of a sense of peace thinking I had comforted him and changed his linens, I left the room, confident the other nurses did not know how to handle him. I left telling him I would be back in a little while to check on him. He was clean and looked as if he understood me. I left thinking I had done a great job.

Later coming back into the room, I quietly entered thinking he was asleep. Boy was I wrong! He coyly peered from his sheets pulled up to his eyes.

The whole room was splattered with his feces. All over the linens, on the floor, on the walls. He had managed to throw it all over and the room was a disaster. I looked in total disbelief! As I was getting over the shock and speaking to him, I cleaned up the mess, explaining to him what he had done, and the importance of him to ring for me to assist. He looked into my eyes like he understood. I placed the ringer in his hand and left.

About thirty minutes later I returned to check on him again. Quietly I opened the door and to my dismay again found the room covered in feces! Walls, linens, on his face and hands, everywhere. Oh my gosh! Now I understood what the other nurses were trying to tell me. I guess I thought I could do something to make things better, different. But I realized at that moment the only thing besides managing the situation and cleaning him up was to pray for him because his mind had been so damaged from the gunshot wound, he was no longer able to respond as a human being.

This young man was really having an experience of being between heaven and hell! Like a purgatory of sorts and all the medical staff had to be a part of it. But thank goodness we were able to remove ourselves from the nightmare at the end of our shift.

7

A Miracle

MY PURSE LOST IN THE SNOW

This experience was very personal. It happened during a trip with my husband to Mammoth Mountain for a ski trip. Tons of snow already covered the mountain. Driving up late in the evening, we had to stop on the way to put chains on the tires. We had heard a huge storm was approaching and that we could get snowed in, but we were young enough to want to go anyway and excited about this adventure. Snow was falling hard by the time we reached the top of the mountain village and our hotel. Ten to fifteen feet of snow had been plowed to the side of the road and several more feet accumulated on the roads. It was very late, and the snow trucks were out and about with their lights glaring in the night. We could barely get out of the car and make our way into the warm inn where we were to stay. The wind was howling and I felt as if we were in Alaska.

After settling into our room, we decided to get something to eat but conditions outside were very difficult—way too dangerous to think of driving anywhere and nothing in the hotel. We made the decision to walk in the blizzard to a Mexican restaurant down the road about a block. I had a little bit of a headache and nausea. I thought I was just hungry. We walked with difficulty to the restaurant, holding on to each other for dear life. It was freezing cold and very windy, the wind blasting with snow that stuck to our eyelashes and faces.

I told my husband I felt so sick I could not finish dinner. That was very rare for me! I realized I was experiencing altitude sickness. So, we decided to walk back to the restaurant in the blizzard. We stumbled back together with me leaning completely on my spouse. Back at the hotel I was so sick and could barely get into bed. I told my husband that if I still felt like this in the morning, there'd be no skiing for me, that I'd want off the mountain. He agreed.

The next morning, I still felt terrible, so we were going home. As I gathered my things, I realized my purse was missing, Oh no! I dropped my shoulder bag in the snow drift that was now plowed to sixteen to eighteen feet high on the side of the road. I told the manager and gave them my information in case anyone found my purse. I knew it was looking very bleak for anyone to find it. We did look but even our car was now covered in three feet of snow!

I was so sad and besides having my credit cards and my checkbook in it (not to mention the lovely hand-tooled bag a friend had made for me), it had all the latest pictures of our first grandchild! Feeling just awful nearly the whole trip and now my lost purse. My stomach sank.

I started to have a conversation with the Lord. It wasn't so much the material things but losing those pictures of our baby grandson was so unsettling. I said this was what was really important to me!

Back in Los Angeles, I started the task of canceling my credit cards, but I really learned my lesson to never carry a checkbook! I had to call the bank every few days to see if anyone used my checks. It was always a no for weeks. After a month of doing this, I let it all go!

This whole situation took place in March. After one-and-a-half months I received a package in the mail. It was my beautiful bag with everything in it! No note, no return address. There inside, my beautiful grandson's baby pictures, the checkbook, and all the credit cards! The snow had melted, and a wonderful person found my purse and mailed it to me. But I see it as a gift to an answered prayer.

8

Strange Encounter

KILLER ON HIS CHEST TATTOO

Upon arriving at the nursing office early in the morning in Kansas City, I was told I would be going to the inner city to see several patients. My supervisor was mainly concerned about one patient: a young man staying with his mother in a blighted area. He was in his twenties. He had recently been released after several years in prison. Late one evening a car had hit him while he danced in the street with friends, and he was now in a wheelchair. I was to go and check on his living conditions, check his general health, and change a super-pubic catheter in his stomach that allowed him to urinate.

I was informed to be careful due to the location, but we nurses were very used to going into dangerous and even gang areas in the city. It was also snowing heavily outside with about two to three feet of snow on the ground, and it was not easy to get around!

Finding the three buildings lined up on the block, I could see there were no markings or numbers on most of the buildings. No snow had been plowed, and you could not see the sidewalks. This was not uncommon for poorer areas of the city. The snow was not cleared like other areas of the city. I noticed a lot of the windows had been boarded up and looked as if many of the apartments were empty. I needed to be cautious and alert in this neighborhood! Quite an experience for a girl from San Clemente, California, and former Miss Laguna Beach!

I sat in my car as I always did and took a deep breath, said a prayer of preparation, grabbed my nursing bag (which I called my Mary Poppins bag), and off I went into this new adventure.

I was knee deep in snow and there was not one mark in the snow. No signs of life! Not even a rabbit trail. It was so quiet and still, and I thought that even in this bad neighborhood how beautiful the stillness was, the white blanket of calm like the hand of the Divine covering the landscape. I took a guess and went to the first building, making a trail in the snow as I tread through. I found boarded windows, no numbers. I knocked on the door on the bottom floor. No answer. The patient's mother had told me they were on the bottom floor apartment. I started out into the snow again, carrying my bag—which was getting heavier by the minute—and me getting warmer dressed in a hat, gloves, coat and layers. It was very uncomfortable.

I dragged through the snow to the next building and came to the lower outside hallway, again boarded windows accept one. I could see slightly into the window and saw a light on. I knocked on the door. A frail woman in maybe her forties answered the door. She was very sweet and humble and seemed grateful I was there to help her son. I noticed a Bible on a small table with a soft light glowing down on the open pages. The apartment was warm but minimally furnished. The mother stated she had been living here on her own until her son got out of prison and started to live with her after being in prison for almost seven years. Now after this horrid accident, she had to take care of all his needs daily and she was really worn out. I looked deep into her eyes and felt a deep compassion of love bathing over us. She escorted me to M's room where there was a hospital bed, a wheelchair, and a bedside commode. He was still in his bed and wanted to get up into his wheelchair. This was no small young man! He was about six feet tall and around 200 pounds. Oh Lord, how is this little woman going to take care of him, I thought? Well, one step at a time and take a deep breath. I was there to not only take care of the catheter and check his vital signs, but to also assess the whole situation and report back as to what their needs were, and then like a warrior spirit with help from above, to fight like living hell to cry out, speak out to those in charge, seeking the help needed for their lives. Could I fix it all? No! But I could make a difference with some much-needed help and assessment. I have seen so much support for the poor and the indigent in Kansas and Missouri. They really make a great effort in providing in their communities.

I introduced myself to this young man and made an eye contact. I saw softness and pain in this patient. We were strangers, and I was coming into his private space and was going to touch him and get very personal with him about his life. I tried to break the ice and asked him questions about his life situation and how he had gotten there. He seemed to warm up to me and answered my questions. Opening his shirt, I was suddenly taken aback by what I saw tattooed on his chest! *KILLER*. I took a deep breath. "Oh, this is interesting." He said he had gotten that while he was in prison. He would not say why he was in prison but that he did that to protect himself because prison was a really rough place. A place of pure survival. He went on to talk about the drugs and all the control the prisoners have and that it is a big game of control. M. mentioned that before prison, as a young angry black male, many people in the community had helped him. He was given many opportunities in the community. Examples of youth programs at churches, community centers for yoga to teach him to manage his anger and thoughts. He still ended up in prison!

He stated that after being released recently he was out in the street in the neighborhood partying with friends on a balmy summer night, blasting music and having fun. (I am sure drinking and whatever along with it.)

He was hit by a speeding car and ended up in the hospital, then rehab for over three to four months before his mother was called to come and get him to take care of him. She was frail and weak, showing signs of struggling her whole life with very little to show for her efforts. Now she was taking care of her 200-pound paraplegic son in a run-down apartment. Oh, such sadness filled my heart! But at the same time, I had my spirit inflamed to help!

With the fight on, I was able to engage in this battle at my office for as much help and assistance that could be rallied. I know I did the best I could and it helped make their lives a little better. More than anything, I was able to listen and showed that I cared, which can be the best medicine.

9

Darkness Farthest from the Light
GUNSHOT FROM GANG

So, before I moved from L.A. to Kansas, I took a job with a company that brought in primarily young people who had been in bad accidents and were either paraplegic or quadriplegic. Many were from gunshot wounds and gang related. I was hired as a manager of the department, and I had to supervise five private homes in the community that were owned by this company. A real eye-opening situation for me!

Each house had a staff that ran it twenty-four hours a day. There was a head nurse and three to four other nurses taking shifts to care for these patients who were either bed bound, or wheel bound. All their physical needs had to be addressed along with catheter care of their urine and bowel programs, because they were paralyzed from the neck down or the waist down. Whenever there was a severe infection, IV antibiotics needed to be given.

I had heard rumors that the patients were still involved in gang and drug activities. I also was tipped off that some of the young nurses were being manipulated and doing drug related things for some of these patients. Being the new supervisor, I had to go and see for myself and investigate the problems. I arrived at one of the homes, which was in a very nice neighborhood.

The house was lovely, well-kept and had about four to five bedrooms and three to four baths all set up for these special patients. I announced myself to the staff, and taking one young nurse aside I discussed with her the rumors and asked if she was being asked to do things that made her uncomfortable? Yes, she said, and that she feared for her life and her family. A few of the gang members insisted that they do certain duties, i.e., delivery or pick up of drugs. These are the patient's caregivers, and they all get very close and deeply connected. If the nurse refused, the patient would threaten to harm her or her family! After talking to several others, I asked to be taken into the room of one of these gang members.

As I entered his room, I sensed a heaviness and a nauseated feeling in the pit of my stomach. He was what you call a complete quad and was basically bedridden. Rock music blared to the point that I could not hear his voice when spoken too. I asked him if I could turn down the music and he said no. I went over and turned the music very low. He peered up at me with the most evil dark look. Very piercing! Here in front of me was a very angry young man. The best way I can describe that moment was looking into the eyes of darkness that is very far from any light! The entire room and house had a heaviness and it left me with a sense of uneasiness. I completed my tasks on the patient and tried to be kind but he wanted only to be in control and tried to control me with his comments!

This was a huge problem that existed in all these houses. The company owner was a soft-spoken nurse who had started this business years ago. It had skyrocketed into a huge business but was now out of her control. I went to her and her husband to inform them that their business was now being ruled by gang members. Right under their own noses! They were completely ignorant of it. They stated they did not know what to do about it. Me being a supervisor and responsible for the staff, I made an appointment with the police department. I have to admit I, too, was somewhat alarmed about my welfare.

Arriving at the police department for my appointment I was again alarmed as to the condition of the detective. He was so burned out! I could see it in his eyes and feel it in my solar plexus. The conversation basically went this way. "These companies do not know what they are getting themselves into! They only look at the dollar signs and have no clue of the element they are bringing to their businesses. These are hard core gang members. They were involved in gun warfare and that is why they are quads and paras."

I looked at the officer with great sadness and realized at the moment that I was entangled in a huge mess way beyond me and my capabilities. I had such mixed emotions about the job, helping others and losing a very fat paycheck! Going back to the office I put in my resignation and would leave in two weeks. That was a horrid experience I would like to forget all together, but a true experience of warfare between darkness and light. Darkness, that which is farthest from the Light.

10

The Miraculous
35,000 Feet Up

While working in Kansas City as a home health nurse, my workload, along with all the other nurses and staff, was very overwhelming. There were days I traveled over fifty to sixty miles a day to see five or six patients. Some days were in the back countryside on ranches and farmland. Other days were in the inner city.

I was beyond exhausted so I suggested to my husband, let's take a trip to Puerto Rico for four or five days! It was January so he agreed, and I planned the trip to get away and find peace, rest, and solitude. I booked the trip for the end of February.

A week before our trip, a huge snowstorm hit and many flights were being canceled. I kept checking and so far, all was good. We would leave in a few days with one stop through Dallas, Texas. Half the country was shut down and hundreds of flights canceled due to this storm. Until we actually got into the air, we were nervous. Runways were covered in snow and ice and the plane wings had to be de-iced, which I had not experienced before. It definitely makes you face your mortality and vulnerability.

We finally arrived in Puerto Rico in early afternoon, and it was beautiful, tropical, and our hotel was perfect. As we entered the lobby, salsa music was playing live and the entire atmosphere was amazing and freeing! A real vacation getaway feeling.

The whole five days were wonderful with eating, dancing in the lobby to salsa every night, walking on the beach and all over the island. What a perfect idea to come here! This was many years before COVID, so it was very freeing with minimal restrictions anywhere. The main problem we faced was getting back home and to work. The entire Southeast and Midwest were blanketed in snow and again many flights had been canceled. Talking to my daughter she was very concerned. Kansas had over three feet of snow on the ground. "Mom, I hope you can get home safe and not get stranded in Puerto Rico." I said we are definitely leaving Puerto Rico because I need to get back to work and I knew we could make it at least to Texas. The snowstorm was so bad that thousands were stranded and missing their lives getting back to normal. I was hoping that would not happen to us!

At the airport we were going through security, and there was a woman of Puerto Rican decent, I believe, next to me. She seemed very upset at me because I was not moving fast enough. No words were exchanged, but we both stopped and looked into each other's eyes. I thought, What is your problem, lady? It was early in the morning and I do not move to fast in the morning.

On the plane our seats were towards the middle of the plane and I was sitting in the middle. I snuggled down and laid my head on my husband's shoulder thinking I would go back to sleep. After several hours in the plane, my husband tried to rouse me. He said someone was in trouble and airline crew were asking on the loudspeaker if anyone was a doctor or a nurse. I stood up and looked around. I guess I am it! In the back of the galley, I saw the four or five stewardesses surrounding a young woman way in the back seat and everyone seemed nervous but still quiet and speaking softly to her. "Are you OK? Can you breathe?"

I picked up my pace and approached the young passenger. Standing over the woman, I could see very quickly she was in serious trouble. After thirty-eight years as a nurse and with my background in critical care, I knew instinctively she was in trouble, and we were 35,000 feet up in the air.

I asked the stewardesses to help me get her to the back galley to get her on the floor and elevate her feet. The plane was very small and the galley was even smaller. They announced again if any others with medical knowledge could come and assist. So guess who shows up? The woman who was impatient with me!

"I knew I would see you again," she said.

"What's your background?" I asked. She was married to a doctor in Puerto Rico, but now she does natural healing. "Fine. Please start massaging her legs and pray." Then I turned to the head stewardess and asked for a blood pressure cuff. She'd been talking to the captain; he was asking if we needed to land in Miami.

Miami? Oh my gosh, with 150 people on the plane who wanted to get to Texas and back to their lives, including us. I told the stewardess to tell the captain to hang on a little longer. I was trying to assess the situation by taking her vital signs and giving her Gatorade due to dehydration. It was very chaotic as the other stewardess tried to keep refreshments served to the passengers and remain as calm as possible. The stewardesses were stepping past us in the small galley. I could not get a pulse, and she had extremely low blood pressure. She was almost going into shock, and I knew we were in trouble.

The stewardess reported to the captain about the patient's condition based on what I was saying. Now she was suddenly talking to a doctor on the phone in Miami. All information was relayed to him about her condition. He said for us to fly into Miami to get her the care she needed. I said my prayers internally and said just give me a few more minutes to see if I can get a blood pressure after she tries to drink more. No luck. She was starting to faint and the stewardess reported that to Miami doctor. Then I heard the stewardess say, "You want her to start an IV?" I was shocked to hear this! I did not know airlines carried IV equipment on board. I looked up to the heavens and said inside, "Lord, help me and give me strength." Then I looked at the stewardess and remembered 911 and Flight 93. "Let's rock and roll!"

I opened the kit and started putting everything together. It was like a musician playing with new people but going for it and soon you can play music and understand each other. The crew helped me with everything I needed. I used a large oven mitt from the galley and taped it to her arm under the IV to stabilize it once it was started. The IV with 1000ml of Ringers lactate was hung from a clothes hanger. Oh, but can I tell you the challenge of trying to start an IV on the floor of a small shaking plane 35,000 feet in the air, and a patient going into shock and overweight on top of it! It could only be done through the grace of the Divine. Again, I looked upward and internally, *Only through You*. I knew I only had a one-shot chance! Got it!

With forty years' experience as a nurse, I took a chance with what I thought was going on and opened the IV completely to help hydrate her. There is a danger in that also but we had very little choice. Now the captain was saying we needed to decide whether to go to Miami, and the doctor was also on the line, waiting. She started to wake up almost miraculously! Thank goodness and thank the Above! "Tell the captain to keep going. We have blood pressure and a pulse!" The same information was given to the doctor in Miami. We were continuing our route to Texas.

I sat on the floor, monitoring her, allowing the others who helped to go back to their seats. The stewardesses to back to their jobs. A sense of peace and calm came over the plane. One male stewardess came by, bent down, and whispered to me, "Are you a military triage doctor?"

"No, I'm not and I'm really getting way too old for this kind of excitement!"

I spent about two hours on the floor with this woman and discussed her health. She was only twenty-nine years old, overweight, and had a heart condition. While in Puerto Rico she forgot her heart medication and had become dehydrated from drinking alcohol while on vacation. I discussed all this with her, making suggestions and giving her tips on how to improve her health. She was very open to listening. I then decided it was OK for her to go back to her seat with another IV bag on the cloth hanger. I asked if she was up to it and she agreed. She had left her sister and five-year-old nephew in the middle of the plane and all this time they did not know if she was alive or dying. The stewardess did give her an update once in a while. Also, the entire front of the plane never really knew what was going on in the back except that someone needed help.

She slowly walked back to her seat, and I carried the IV bag. Her sister looked up in disbelief and joy all at the same time. The patient told her nephew that I had saved her life and how grateful she was! He just stared at me in disbelief, then he reached up with his little hand and touched my face.

It was all well worth it, but the amazing experience had left me exhausted. I walked back to my seat with my husband and everyone in the back of the plane softly clapped. Such a amazing humbling moment!

So, we had about one and a half hours before arriving at the Dallas airport. I slipped down deep into my seat and quickly fell asleep on my husband's shoulder. Then on approaching the airport, the captain announced to everyone that most on the plane was aware of a problem with one of the passengers and that everyone should stay in their seats when we land because he would have the paramedics come aboard to remove the sick passenger. I was about eight rows back and I slid deeper into my seat. I just wanted to disappear due to exhaustion. No questions please!

As the plane landed, it was very quiet on the plane. Not one sound being made! The paramedics arrived and were guided back to the sick passenger. I watched what was going on by peering over the seat in front of me. There were two paramedics and the lead was a female. They looked at the IV hanging from the clothes hanger over the passenger's seat with almost a look of astonishment. I could see the disbelief in their faces and eyes. I shrank deeper into my seat!

My husband pushed on my arm and said to me, "They're looking for you!" I looked up and sure enough they seemed to be searching the rows with their eyes. One of the stewardesses came back and said they wanted to talk to me. Oh dear, I guess I have to do it! Walking up to them, they were stern and started to drill me. Maybe they thought I was not a medical person. I identified myself as a forty-year veteran nurse and the decision was made along with a doctor in Miami to start the IV with a quick diagnosis of dehydration, patient going into shock, and a history of a heart condition. They softened a little and looked at me "We just don't see this often where someone starts an IV on a plane 35,000 feet up!" I agreed and even though it was a wonderful experience to save someone and our flight of 150 other people, I hope to never repeat it! I retired one year later!

11

Miracles

TWIN BABIES

My friend had approached me about her niece who was unable to get pregnant. She was in her thirties and her husband was twenty years older. They were all from the Middle East where it is not uncommon to marry older or younger first cousins. She had been trying to get pregnant for years and as she felt her clock was running out. They were now going for all kinds of testing at UCLA in California at the specialty clinic and so far, no luck with anything they had tried.

I asked what their names were and said I would pray for them. We all belonged to the same Christian church. About a week later I called my friend and told her what came to me after prayer early in the morning. "Tell them to take one teaspoon of organic wheat germ oil a day in the morning for at least one month for both the husband and wife." She agreed to relay the information. I had only been aware of them through my nurse friend and their aunt, but I had never met them personally. I also said we should all continue to pray for success. She agreed!

Two months later my friend informed me that they were successful in a new pregnancy! Everyone was so excited, and it was true a miracle with the help of prayer and the wheat germ oil!

Three months into the pregnancy I was informed that all was well with the pregnancy but that they were expecting *twins*! And then another gift! A girl and a boy! Oh my gosh! Amazing gifts!

The staff at UCLA wanted her to bring in the bottle of wheat germ so they could analogize its content. I just laughed when I heard this. These are mysteries of the Supernatural.

When the babies were born, I heard the good news all was well for both of them and the family was beyond joyful! I was invited to a welcome home party at the house. I was really working hard as a home health nurse and lots of weekends, but I accepted because I really wanted to see these babies! Arriving at the house in a lovely neighborhood, gated with a huge, towering glass and iron front door, I thought I was entering a palace. As the door was opened by the young mother, a huge crowd of family and friends of the couple applauded and sang songs of joy around me! I only knew my elderly nurse friend. The party, I was told, was in celebration of me and how I had helped the babies come into the world. I was very humbled and had never expected them to elevate and celebrate me in this way. Another amazing gift and story. I asked to see the beautiful gifts from above and was able to look into their eyes. It truly was a heavenly moment on Earth.

12

The Mysterious

THE DIPLOMATS FROM INDIA

While working in L.A. as a home health nurse, my supervisor asked if I would be interested in doing a special visit out in Malibu. I said sure. This would be interesting and I was always up for an adventure! She informed me the patients were staying at a doctor's home in Malibu. It was quite a drive, and they wanted a nurse who would be sensitive to these traveling dignitaries. I accepted and got on my way after receiving a report that the woman was not well while they had been traveling around the world. My assignment was to take vital signs and to do a blood sample on both the husband and his wife. They were not able to travel to the hospital where the doctor worked. I was informed the doctor had attempted to draw blood from the woman but was unable.

Arriving at the top of a rolling hill in Malibu overlooking the ocean, I noticed a lovely calm feeling as I approached the huge home sitting up on the hill. There were several cars parked at the bottom of the hill. As I walked to the sidewalk suddenly the entire walkway was drawn with beautiful chalk flowers in multiple colors, and on the porch were about twenty pairs of shoes and sandals. I took a deep breath, removed my shoes, and gently knocked on the door. The door opened and a group of mainly woman rushed towards me and surrounded me. They were all dressed in beautiful colored saris and the men were all in white pants and tunics. They circled around me, slowly ushering me into the living room. Asking me to have a seat, one of the women started to ask me questions about if I prayed or meditated? I said yes for many years I have been praying and meditating. They said before I was allowed to be in the presence of the couple, they would like to pray over me. I agreed. It was nice and calming to have them again form a circle and place their hands above my head and shoulders. It reminded me of prayer groups I had been to before.

After a few minutes we all sat together in the living room, waiting for the approved time to see my patients. I was informed the woman was a holy woman in India, and she was highly revered. Her background included working with Gandhi when she was a young woman. Being born in India, she had been raised as a Christian in a mostly Hindu environment. She was called Mother.

I would be seeing her husband first. He was a diplomat of India. I waited. Twenty to thirty minutes went by and then finally someone came for me and asked if I was prepared. I said yes, I was, being a little nervous but confident as to my task. Walking into his room, I and my patient were introduced. He had such gentle eyes, I remember, and was tall and lean with beautiful brown skin. Truly a man of dignity. There was a sense of honor to be there and be asked to take care of these fine visitors. I had him sit down, and I explained what I was going to do. He was kind and obliging. I took his vital signs then was able to obtain the blood sample with no problems. Thanking the Lord with gratitude!

Now that I was finished with him, a service person said, "Now we shall go to Mother. Are you prepared?"

"Yes."

He explained she was very ill with a generalized weakness. I was a little nervous and hoped I would be able to make the right decision about her care. We walked into a huge well-lit master bedroom. She sat in a large lounge chair with her legs up. Long flowing dark hair, dressed in a soft blue sari and a décor of the third eye in the middle of her forehead. Bright red! She was a large woman and very overweight. I was, concerned about the task of drawing blood. Being overweight makes the task more difficult.

Our eyes met and she gently smiled at me and I at her. She never spoke a word to me, but her attendants surrounded and hovered close by her. I introduced myself and explained the task at hand. She nodded with approval. I had to really practice staying in the moment and not being taken by a daunting task. After taking her vital signs, I started to look over her arms and even her legs and feet for a possible vein. We usually do not like drawing blood from someone's feet; it is a little more dangerous. I slowly looked and felt on her arms and legs. Nothing that looked like even a possibility! This patient needed what they call a cut down to get to her vein, and I knew that was beyond my scope! I explained the situation and everyone was disappointed, but I knew I had made the right decision not to try. All my years of experience, I was not going to cause unnecessary pain to this wonderful lady.

I was escorted out of the room and left the home. I looked back and felt a warm glow and thought, this is one of the greatest experiences in my nursing career!

13

Darkness Farthest from the Light

GANG MEMBER QUADRIPLEGIC

After getting my assignment for the day, I was informed I would be going into a gang area in the San Fernando Valley and that I should be careful. As I said before this is not unusual for nurses in home health; we are used to these areas. I must admit I like the excitement and the challenge of doing something adventurous! My patient was also a gang member, and he had an abdominal wound of the stomach, which I would be changing the dressing.

As I drove into the gang area called a ghetto, I noticed tennis shoes thrown along an electric wire crossing the street above my head like a gateway going into the ghetto. I knew this was a sign because another nurse had told me about it and that it was a warning of the gang's territory.

I pulled in front of the cute little Spanish house, which was simple and covered with flowers and a vegetable garden that filled the entire yard.

Walking up to the door I heard a loud barking dog, a Pitbull. A lot of the ghettos like to have these dogs because they can be trained to be mean even though they are a great breed of dog. At the screen door, he barked viciously at me and jumped up against the door. His teeth show with a wide mouth. I stood back and was cautious, and as he jumped higher and harder, the screen started to open! In that moment, one of the owners grabbed his collar and hauled him away. Greatly to my relief!

I introduced myself and stated I was there to see the young patient. They were waiting for me to come and were grateful for help. With the dog put safely away, I followed the gentleman, who said he was a brother, down the dark hallway. The house was clean and had a warm feeling to it with a smell in the air of a savory Mexican soup cooking. Coming into his bedroom, I noticed a handsome young man around seventeen or eighteen years old lying in a hospital bed with no shirt on, just covered with a sheet. A large bandage covered his whole abdomen, and he was a paraplegic, paralyzed from the waist down, from his injuries. You have to realize I was coming into someone's home whom I had never met before nor he me, and I was going to do some very intimate tasks and procedures on him. I had to dig deep to find an openness and show a nonjudgmental attitude to be allowed in his space. The truth is I really did care and people can usually feel that from you.

I introduced myself and told him I was going to check his wound, change his dressing on the gunshot wound, and take his vital signs. He agreed to allow me to do those tasks.

He was such a sweet young man and so warm hearted that it was hard to believe he was a gang member. As we talked and got to know each other, I asked about the shoes at the entrance of his neighborhood. He stated, "Oh those are other gangs' shoes that we have shot, and we throw them up there as a warning to stay away from our turf!" I took a deep breath not believing what I had just heard.

Before I started to change his dressing, I asked, "Do you have any of your buddies coming by today?" He said yes that he expected a few to be by shortly. I could feel the blood rush up to my cheeks. I needed to hurry up and get the heck out of there before they came by for a visit.

I checked his vital signs and completed his dressing change and was just getting all my things put back in my bag when suddenly two tough-looking young men pushed the door open. The whole atmosphere changed instantly. This sweet young man suddenly changed his entire attitude. The best way to describe it is he had an attitude. He was a person showing how he was so tough and nothing fazes him. I said hello to them, and they just looked into my eyes coldly with same dark attitude. I had to get out right away because I did not want to be a part of this cold dark game being played in front of me. They had proven to me, quite well, that the dark game of control-and-take was a serious one.

14

Mystery and Miracle

ALLIE, TOO YOUNG TO DIE

This event happened while working as a home health nurse in L.A. in my mid-forties. Our neighbor had informed us their young daughter in her thirties was diagnosed with advanced breast cancer. She was a mother of two young children. One was under the age of two. So very sad, but I see lots of sad terrible cases. To tell you the truth, I was not close to her but my daughter was very close to her. Of course, I could feel the pain of the family and it was not good news. They informed me she was in the hospital and had very little time left. Could I please let my daughter know. She now lived in Kansas.

Calling my youngest daughter to inform her of her friend's condition was not an easy task. She was very upset to say the least. My daughter said, "I will pray for her, Mother," then hung up the phone.

The next day my daughter called. "Mom, I had a dream about Allie and in the dream the message was 'Tell her to look to the light.' Mom, will you go give her my love and give her that message?"

I had great resistance to doing that because first of all, I was working so hard as a nurse and the last thing I wanted to do was go to a hospital to see a young dying girl that I really did not have a good relationship with! But loving my daughter and knowing her faith, I agreed to do it the next day after work.

The next day of work was unbelievably busy. I had a huge patient load and had to drive fifty to sixty miles, so I was thinking I couldn't get to the hospital as planned.

When I got home around five or six p.m., I was beyond exhausted with the heat index over 108 degrees. I came home and lay on the couch, thinking it is humanly impossible to go to the hospital tonight. I remember telling my husband I did not think I could do it.

I had dinner after a while and then returned to the couch, still barely able to move and fell asleep. While sleeping I had a dream and a voice said very clearly to me, "You must go to Allie and give the message!" I know I was dreaming but it was very clear! I got up and told my husband where I was going.

I dragged myself to the car. By now it was dark outside. I knew I still had a few more hours for the hospital to be open to visitors. I headed out to a not very good part of town, but I was used to that. I had in my tired mind an idea how to get there. I had never been to this huge community hospital.

I got lost in a very dark industrial area, and we had no GPS then, it was all done on paper maps. I pulled under the freeway to look at my map and try to calm down and not panic. It was as if every negative force was against me! Here I was in a dark underpass at night alone. I checked to make sure my doors were locked. As I was trying to focus, centering myself in prayer and asking for help, I look up and saw two young men sitting at the other end of the underpass, headlights off and staring right at me! I was scared and prayed out loud. "Lord, help me." I drove onto the ramp as fast as I could, not knowing if I made the right decision but at least I was away and safe! I drove for about five to ten minutes. I looked to my right and there on the hill all lit up was the hospital. Now that was amazing! I got there.

I want you to understand I was moving with great resistance. I was really doing this from the love of my daughter, and I felt I was listening to a Higher messenger!

I went to the information desk and got directions to Allie's room. It was quiet in the hospital because it was late, close to 7:45 and no visitors after 8:00. Oh, I do not want to be here! I thought to myself.

I waited somewhat anxiously outside the door until the nurse would come out. In my heart I knew I had to attempt at giving the message my daughter presented to me and through my dream. The message was: Allie, don't be afraid of the dark! Look to the Light!

The nurse came out and I introduced myself as a nurse and a friend of Allie.

She informed Allie that she had a visitor. I slowly walked in and she looked at me, shocked and almost staring at me like "Why are you here, lady?" I really understood that. Here she was bald and sick, and I had no real relationship with her. "Nikki wanted me to come and see you and bring you her love." I felt very awkward and in the deep part of my ordinary self, I thought, There is no way I am going to deliver this message.

I went over and sat by her in the chair as she crawled back into bed. Hearing my daughter had cared about her enough to send a message was comforting to her. We spoke about my daughter and her relationship, and a little more comfort settled in. It was Holy Thursday and Easter would be on Sunday. I asked, "So, what do you think of all that is going on with you?"

She looked right into my eyes and said, "Oh, I am doing fine and will be home with my family and kids for Easter!" She was in complete denial, and obviously, being a young mother of two young children, she was not prepared to die. It was all so sudden. I was bold enough to ask her about her faith but she referred only to loving her family. Now I was thinking there is no way I could deliver this message. I felt disappointed and started to prepare to say goodbye and leave. I slowly got up and walked to the foot of her bed, touching her feet as I said goodbye for my daughter and me. As I did that, she suddenly said, "Please don't turn out the light! I am afraid of the dark!" A surge of energy came through me and I said loudly and boldly, "Allie, do not be afraid of the dark! Look to the Light." She looked up at me and stared as if shocked but also comforted.

She died the very next day on Good Friday. I found out from her family that she was always afraid of the dark.

15

A Miracle

MAN AT THE GYM

I was in a place of real searching for more meaning in my life and work! An even deeper spiritual connection with my work. The nursing work I had been doing for thirty-some years had put me on this journey, this quest of being open to more and a more profound longing to do a deeper work. Working with a greater awareness and attention. I was questioning the present job I had and was wondering if I should stay. I was working in a holistic clinic as a nurse consultant but I had a desire to go back out into the community to see regular people and the indigent. The clinic was wonderful, but I was dealing primarily with the rich and some were very demanding.

So, on my next day off I decided to get in touch with my deeper self and be very quiet and listen carefully. I had also decided to go to the gym to have some self-time and exercise and be alone. As I drove up to the gym, I said a prayer and asked to be shown direction in regard to all I was feeling.

Walking into the gym I noticed a man very short of breath sitting to my right. I slowed down to observe him, watching and being cautious as to whether I should interfere. I walked up to him and asked if he was all right. He said he was OK. I could see he was not OK. "I'm a nurse and I can see you are not OK. Can I take your pulse?"

He agreed. It was racing and he was getting more short of breath!

"I'm going to call 911 if that is all right."

Again, he agreed.

I ran to the desk and asked them to call 911 and told them what was going on. He called and said they would be here in a minute because they were right next door to the gym. I stayed by his side and rubbed his back gently. I suddenly had a wave of compassion move over me, so I started to say a silent prayer for his healing and well-being! The paramedics arrived and I explained the situation and they took over, checking all his vital signs. I said goodbye and he and the paramedics thanked me. As I turned away, I looked back and he was showing a little more distress so they laid him down. I went on into the gym, knowing I had done my part. I expected them to rush him to the hospital. Having a background as a cardiac nurse, I knew he was in trouble!

I worked out for about an hour and was walking back through the lobby when I saw a female paramedic standing there and no patient. I was shocked and did not understand. I asked what happened and wondered where the man had gone. She said after I left, he suddenly sat up and felt great. He was no longer short of breath and all his vital signs stabilized so he went and showered. "We are still going to drive him to his regular MD to be checked but no hospital trip!"

I was really in shock! All my years as a nurse I knew he was in serious trouble. To me this was the sign I was looking for, the power of prayer and compassion for another. I know we were helped with Divine intervention. It was good he went to MD for follow up, but he was fine now, and I got my answer and gave my notice to leave the job I was at and go back into the field to help the indigent in the city and country.

16

The Mysterious
MAGICAL PEACOCKS IN MY YARD

I had worked in the hospital for over twelve years, first as a CNA then as an RN, ICU/CCU nurse. The last five years had been in the ICU/CCU units.

I was very tired of the hospital environment and decided to go into home health care to really be with the people and be in their environment. I felt I was experienced enough to be able to make the necessary decisions on my own and work with the doctors from their offices directly with their patients.

Around 1986 I started working with the Visiting Nurses Association, which had been around for a long time. I went through a six-week orientation with other nurses, which is unheard of nowadays. After this I was sent out on my own. Exciting but scary at the same time. All the decisions I had to make using my years of experience and, of course, I could always call the office of my supervisor or the MD office for any orders or suggestions.

One of my first patients I will never forget! I had to go to a very old but beautiful area in Van Nuys, California. Most of the houses were ranch style on large one acre lots. Most seemed to have animals or horses on the property. Lots of eucalyptus trees and very lovely.

I was having a hard time finding my patient's property. Remember, no GPS, no cell phones.

Going up and down the street, I could only figure out that the old house in the middle of street with no number on the mailbox must be the one. It was very different than the other houses. The majority were built maybe thirty or forty years ago but this was at least a one-hundred-year-old wooden cabin looking like something out of a scary fairy tale like Hansel and Gretel.

The driveway was all gravel with weeds growing everywhere. It was a circular drive so I pulled up in front of the door. The windows you could not see through; they were made of glass over one-hundred years ago, thick like coke bottles. Several cats walked inside that I could barely make out. This was scary and adventurous! I have always had that in me.

The doorknob was a circle ring, huge, and there was a large iron knocker in the middle of the solid wood door. The house was a log cabin.

I knocked on the door, no answer. Then knocked over and over again. I needed to get in and give her gold shots for arthritis. I heard a shuffling sound and an old woman's scary voice, "Who is it?"

"The nurse to give you your shot," I yelled back. More shuffling toward the door. My imagination was running wild at this point, but I tried to stay centered and took a deep breath. She was barely able to open the creeping door. There before me stood the things made of nightmares. She was in her nineties, hunched over, wearing a long cape type of shawl, with long grey hair past her shoulders.

"Come in. Want to see my animals?" She was very friendly.

"Sure," I said with some hesitation. It was like stepping back into time! Well over one-hundred years of it! Cats ran off the windowsill and jumped to the floor to surround me. Maybe five or six of them. I had to step over lettuce thrown on the floor, and there were three huge tortoises crawling around. The smell was not good! I was wanting to get my job done and get the heck out of there because I could not breath well!

I had a hard time finding a place to put my bag down.

My patient could only talk about her animals and how important they were to her. As I scanned the crowded dusty old room, it was like being in the 1800s. This place was made of all logs with a huge fireplace in the middle of the room. There was a large metal pot hanging in the middle of the fireplace. I looked around the room and saw very old pictures hanging of the walls and asked if I could look. She was very excited to share.

"Now this one is with Clark Gable. I taught him how to ride horses back when he was a very young star in Hollywood." She was right! There he was on a horse in the backyard, her backyard. Wow!

I was in the twilight zone; this was quite an adventure, but I still wanted to get out after I gave her the gold shot I was there to give. I gave her the shot for her arthritis, and she was calm and reflective.

"I've lived here my whole life and still mow my whole property. I love my animals. I'd just die without them and now the city is trying to get rid of all my outside animals!"

I had a real moment of compassion for her but said I had to leave now. She insisted I go outside with her before I leave, saying "Want to see my birdies?"

"Birdies? Sure, why not?"

We stepped over the turtles and outside to the patio. There was a mess of food on the floor and lettuce and turtle poo everywhere. But also a huge dachshund weighing in at about sixty to seventy pounds. His hind legs were paralyzed so he was dragging himself around on the floor with his tail wagging and trying to catch up with us! I was in a daze and speechless just looking and looking around me at this life before me. I was trying not to judge; actually, everything was happening so fast I did not have time to judge. Also in this screened porch was a gigantic lighted hatchery full of huge eggs. Could I believe my eyes? What the heck were they? They were huge! I was staring at the lighted shelves in disbelief, watching, and suddenly before I could ask what kind of eggs, I heard a loud screeching sound in the backyard. I looked up and saw an enormous white peacock in front of the screen door with all his plumes open in full glory and making such a lot of noise and showing off to say here I am look at me! *Oh my gosh those are peacock eggs! She raises peacocks in her house and backyard.*

This was like being in a Disney movie, my chest filling with joy and excitement. No wonder she loves it here and all her animals with the lovely trees over one-hundred feet high and the smell of eucalyptus everywhere. I stepped out into the fresh air and it was as if I went through a process to get to Treasure Island. As I slowly looked around me in awe and utter amazement, slowly there were over maybe ten peacocks, all opening their feathers and wearing their crowns, saying, here I am, look at me!

DAILY MIRACLES AND ENCOUNTERS

The process of finding my patient's house, going through the horrid messy, smelling house led me here! I felt as if I was in heaven and will never forget that day of enduring, caring, and coming to such a magical experience. This was such a wonderful learning and growth experience that taught me not to judge anyone but to enjoy the gift given me to help and share their lives and personal joys and environment.

17

Unnerving

Dangerous Blue Eyes

I was taking an extensive computer class after I started with a new home health agency in Kansas City. I had tried to avoid the laptop computer for many years because I am not tech savvy, but Kansas City is very tech savvy so no more could I avoid it! The training went on for three weeks and I would leave each class exhausted and sometimes in tears!

The second week, the class had started very early because I had patients to see in the late morning. I believe it ran from 7:30 to 9:00 a.m. Every class I dreaded so again I left feeling a little upset and exhausted. As I was pulling out of the driveway from the covered parking lot, a young man stepped off the curb directly in front of my car and he hit the hood of my car with his fist in anger. Oh my gosh! I was so sorry as I looked at him and mouthed those words. He was shirtless with a bandanna on his head and his jacket wrapped around his hips. I noticed him stumbling toward my window, and he started to pound on my window, making an effort to talk to me. Well, I had worked in the inner city for many years so I was hoping not to be stupid but thought I should hear what he had to say with caution. I mindfully put my finger on the window lever, thinking I will keep my finger on this button just in case he was not going to be friendly.

Slowly I lowered the window about four or five inches to hear him and as soon as I did him thrust his hand and arm through the window. I immediately pulled back, quickly avoiding his hand from grabbing my neck! I was able to press the button fast on the window, so it locked his arm in place while I stayed pushed almost to the other side of the front seat.

He started to scream, "Let me go! Let my arm go! You are hurting me!"

I looked directly into his eyes. "Do you promise to stop and take it out?"

"Yes!"

I stared at him. His arm and hand were turning color and it must have hurt. I slowly lowered the window and as soon as he felt the release, he went for my throat again.

"I am going to hurt you and I want sex!"

I again jammed his arm and hand and held it as hard as I could. Now he was really screaming. "Stop, stop, OK, I will take it out!"

This time I looked even more intently into his blue eyes. "You had better and you promise?" He knew I meant business and was not playing his game. Slowly I rolled down the window, this time not taking my eyes away, glaring into his! Then in a moment he turned around and ran fast down the street. It was obvious he was on some sort of drug and looked as if he was affiliated with a gang in the area.

Concerned about other people, I called 911 to report the incident and give a good description of the intruder.

I told the operator what had occurred and she repeated to me in shock. "You did what'? She was in disbelief that I had rammed his arm and hand in my car window. Almost breathless she said she would send the police to check on me and look for him.

"No need. I am off to see my patients, and he is running down the road, but thank you! I just think the police should stop and check on him, so he does not scare another person."

After giving a complete description of him and what he was wearing, I told her, "And he had the most beautiful blue eyes! So sad!"

18

The Mysterious to a Miracle

ON MY WATCH IN CCU, MAN AWAKENS

I had been a nurse for about four years and working in ICU/CCU at a hospital in LA when this extraordinary event took place. My specialty and favorite place in the hospital was CCU, the cardiac unit. It was an even-paced part of the hospital but could be exciting when something happened.

I was an on-staff RN who had a flexible schedule because I had a young family. I would usually work the 3–11 p.m. shift two to three days a week, which also included lots of Saturdays. This way I could have my children taken care of and not be away for long periods of time. Because I had a flexible schedule, I was considered a float nurse. They would send me where they needed me between ICU and CCU but also at times anywhere in the hospital even pediatrics or on the surgical floor, which was a nice change of pace if you are flexible.

Because the staff knew I was flexible and not full-time, many times I would get really sick and complicated cases. Even patients that were not expected to live during the shift. Because I loved my job and did have so much flex, I tried never to complain about that.

This night was one of those nights! We ICU/CCU nurses usually never had more than two patients in those units because of all the problems, medications, and IVs involved with the very sick and critical ones. I was given report and told that this man, Mr. B., had had a massive heart attack almost a week ago. CCU staff had been trying to save his life and had tried everything they knew. He was in a coma and not responsive; he was being kept alive with medications and IVs. He was breathing on his own so he was not on a ventilator but there was no hope for his recovery. My job as a nurse was to slowly remove all the tubing and his general bedside care and inform the family in the lobby of what we were doing. I was to inform them that we were taking him off all the equipment and we did not expect him to make it. *Oh my gosh! How sad and I am the one chosen for this difficult privilege.*

Mr. B was in his sixties, still very young as far as I felt. After introducing myself as his nurse for the next shift, I informed his wife waiting in the lobby what I was going to do. She said she understood and that the doctors had informed her of the needed process.

As I walked back to Mr. B., I felt overwhelmed with compassion for the family, patience, and myself! I started with my internal prayers asking the Divine to guide me and give me strength to do my part at the end of the *mysterious to a miracle*. I moved slowly around his bed, being quiet and respectful, internally saying prayers for Mr. B. as I removed all the IVs and tubes from his body. This took time and I kept checking the monitors and watching his vital signs fluctuate. His blood pressure would get lower and lower, then his heart rate would speed up and then go down. All the signs of a person letting go of their life. The compassion and sadness were all very real and intense! Now as I was removing the last tubes, I thought how I would allow the family to come in until his passing and allow their time with him. The emotion swelled up inside of me, to an almost intolerable level. As I removed the last tubes from his body, I noticed a stirring in him. I heard his wife crying and coming to the door of his room and suddenly she cried out "Henry, I love you!" His eyes opened and he turned his head towards his wife's voice. She fell on his chest sobbing in tears of joy. He had awakened!

A true miracle! Everyone was in shock, including me! The doctors were called and examined him. Mr. B. went home a few days later with his family. Of course, most of the staff said he was over sedated with medication. And many teased me for a while that I brought somebody back from the dead, but everyone really knew it was a miracle!

19

Mysterious Encounter

400-POUND PATIENT WON'T GET OUT OF BED

I was given my morning assignment and was warned by my supervisor that one of my patients was very difficult. She was a bedbound woman in her sixties who lived alone and had given up on life. Obese, diabetic, incontinent of bowels and urine. Her entire family had disowned her and she had used up all her friends and burnt out most help and nurses who went to see her.

Wow! This will be a real challenge.

On my way, I wondered how she ate her food. How did she clean herself? As I arrived, I sat in my car preparing myself and centered on prayer and quietness as I always do. This helped me to be more balanced with all this running across my mind. I approached the small middle class brown house that was in much need of repair.

During a phone call, the patient told me the front door would be open, she would be in the back bedroom, and not to worry about her two Chihuahuas dogs that would be protecting her on her bed. Oh dear! What was I up against?

I knocked on the door and heard a voice in the back room. The two dogs began to bark loudly.

"Come on in, the dogs will not hurt you!" she yelled out in a friendly voice.

I cautiously entered. The house was very dark, musty, and had bad air ventilation. I walked down a dark hallway with great anticipation as to what I was going to find.

As I entered her room, I was shocked at what I saw.

Before my eyes was a woman about 400 plus pounds, balding thin red hair, sitting in a lotus position, two yelping Chihuahuas on her shoulders. She was naked from the waist down and a brown striped poncho covered her top.

I noticed a small refrigerator on her right side and bookshelves stacked to the ceiling. I was amazed that there seemed to be a little order in the room. She was in a king bed that took up most of the room with only a few feet on either side of the bed which was close to a sliding glass door going out into a messy yard.

She was very friendly at first because it was our first meeting, but after a few medical questions I could see and hear the unrest and her temper escalating. She wanted everything her way and was very demanding. I informed her I was there to take her vital signs and give her a shot for an infection she had.

The patient soon revealed her true nature and she had played this game many times trying to manipulate many people. She informed me she wanted me to clean her. She was sitting in feces and urine, and after that she wanted me to get her lunch from the refrigerator, etc. She had no respect for me, that I was a nurse. She only saw a person to get her what she needed in the most manipulative way and at any cost.

I got her game right away and knew I was dealing with a very psychotic person. This time I let her work me a little, and since I was trying to develop a relationship with her I pretty much did what she asked of me because this was her life. As nurses we run into this on occasion, but we are usually used mainly for our high level of skills, for IVs, injections, wound care and general assessment of patient condition and making recommendations for the needs in the home like cleaning, bathing, etc.

The problem with Betty was she burned everyone, and they did not want to come back. As I was attending to her and cleaning her up, having her roll from side to side, the dogs would just go with the flow and stay on her shoulders. Not to be cruel, but it was almost comical, and we nurses must keep a sense of humor to survive! Just imagine changing a diaper on a 400-plus baby! It was good that I was in great health and strong from my many years of yoga.

Attending to her, she had me running around and doing this and that for her. I told her I was going to get her a bath person, and if possible, help from my office for her food, etc. Talking to her, I heard the front door open and this small girl with dark skin came in looking exhausted. I found out she had helped Betty in the past but quit the job because of the abuse but stopped by daily at the end of the day from her other job to make sure she had food or to clean her up. Oh my gosh! What an angel. I could never be that dedicated. I wanted to help, but I also wanted to help teach patients to be responsible and not to manipulate.

Finishing up the day with Betty, I asked if the girl would talk to me outside for a few moments. She agreed. I said my goodbyes and said I would be back in a few days and walked out the door with the helper.

I asked her questions about what she knew about Betty's family and her life. She explained Betty had been a high-level teacher of literature and spoke several languages. After many years of teaching, her weight increased and increased and her family said one day she just gave up on life. Her husband and two grown children disowned her after many years of this going to bed and manipulating everyone. Now she did it to anybody who came in the front door—service men, gas men, handymen—to get her food and even clean her up. "She has no shame!"

I went back to my office and arranged for all the home assistance care I could get her through her insurance. I felt pretty good at my accomplishment and that I was being a good nurse trying not to be overly judgmental.

I went back a few days later. I again arrived early in the morning and was happy to inform Betty of others coming to help. She went into a rage with me because the bath aide had not come, and she was furious, so I agreed to bathe her. I had trouble keeping the dogs off her naked 400-pound body as I attempted to sponge bathe her and clean up the poo she was sitting in. My continual prayer was "Lord, give me strength," which I said inwardly. I was doing my very best under the circumstances and nothing was good enough.

She started yelling at the top of her voice, very much verbal abuse, and I do not do well with that. I informed her to stop the abuse, or I would leave and not come back.

She continued!

I left the room with her sitting in a lotus position, naked and screaming with the two dogs sitting like guards on her shoulders, not making a sound. I ran out the front door and stood in the driveway wondering what to do? As a nurse I cannot abandon the patient. I would lose my license. I stood holding my arms across my chest almost to protect myself from the screaming assault. She continued to scream and yell and curse obscenities! I stood my ground and allowed her to continue to vent and cry like a child. She was now helpless and naked. After about ten minutes, the crying started to soften, and I opened the door and asked her if she was going to calm down and be kinder. She agreed and I agreed to come and finish her bath and get her clothes and feed her.

I realized in that moment that this was way above my capabilities as a nurse. I went into this profession to help and console and use my highly trained skills to help heal. This patient had such a wounded heart and soul and such mental issues it was going to take a very special person to help her to regain her life.

I returned to my office and informed them I would not go back. She did receive another nurse's case manager and some home assistance. I have no idea if any lasted more than a week.

Never give up on life. To lose hope is to lose life!

20

Miracle

NO AUTISM FOR THIS LITTLE TWO-YEAR-OLD BOY

When we made the tremendous move from L.A. to Kansas in 2005, it was a huge undertaking to say the least! We gave most away and had the few things we kept shipped by truck. We loaded our car and moved to Kansas to live with our daughter and family until we found our own home. We had been visiting the Midwest for over sixteen years and I really thought I would like it and could live there.

I did not work as a nurse for about three months, taking my time to get used to the new life. My daughter shared different things about her life and about her friends that I really enjoyed hearing and sharing, especially after being apart for so long. One story she occasionally shared was about a not very close friend but someone she cared about very much. She said she was very private and had three boys but had mentioned on the phone that the youngest one seemed to have issues and was a little "off." I immediately thought of autism because it was such an issue and I had worked closely in L.A. with a group of chemists and pharmacists who were trying to figure out what was going on and why so many children had been affected. One thing that had been discovered especially in integrative medicine was the use of thimerosal (mercury) as a preservative for most vaccines.

I paid attention but did not get into that complex discussion with my daughter. I was trying to get my life together. Months later my daughter brought it up again and her concern over her friend secluding herself. She mentioned again about problems with her little boy. I just listened with concern myself.

After about a year, I had started a job at a holistic clinic and was working as an assistant for a clinical nutritionist and pharmacist. We were dealing with these problems and concerns with people all over the US and I was learning so much in the way of more natural uses of healing. We dealt with children with autism and saw improved results by doing many natural things to help them.

After I'd been at the clinic for a year, my daughter again mentioned her friend and confided that he had been diagnosed with autism. She and her family were just devastated, and she expressed her frustration to my daughter, saying the doctors kept telling her there was nothing wrong, but she knew better so she pursued finding a doctor who would listen to her. That night I had a dream, and in the dream, I was told that I could help this woman and her little boy! The next day I told my daughter about the dream and to please have her friend call and make an appointment at the clinic to discuss his case and that I thought we could help him. It was sort of strange, but I told her the dream was very clear and vivid!

In a few weeks I got a call at the clinic, and she had made an appointment. The mother came in by herself and we discussed her little boy and all his symptoms and what she had been given to help him. She said nothing was given and how he was overactive, did not sleep well, had poor focus, etc. I told her I would get back to her after a discussion with the clinical nutritionist and her suggestion for his program. After a long review, I was given a program the mother should follow for two weeks and report back to me with any problems or concerns. The program included natural things to help remove any mercury from his system and balance his nutrition with good foods and not preservatives or additives in his food.

After about one week I was driving home from work exhausted and got a phone call from his mother. She was very upset and almost crying!

"He is worse and now wetting his bed more! I can't continue with this."

I turned inward and stayed quiet because in my heart and mind I knew he was detoxing from the mercury. Because he was little, I told her to half the dose of everything and then call me in a few days. She agreed.

I lost a lot of sleep and said lots of prayers, then I got the call in a few days, and all was good. The mother said he was doing amazing and was a changed child!

"Great. Continue with the program and call us in a month or two."

Two months passed and we heard nothing. Then one day at work someone came to get me and said someone was here to see me. I walked out and saw it was the young mom.

"My doctor just informed me that there are no signs of any autism. He has been perfect." Then she reached down to her son. "Sam, say hi to the nice lady that helped you." This beautiful little three-year-old boy peered from around her legs. He was so adorable with thick brown hair and dark clear brown eyes and stared at me in wonderment.

What a joy and one of the greatest gifts I have ever experienced in my life and given direction from ABOVE!

21

The Mysterious

WOMAN AND LITTLE INVISIBLE CHILD

The elderly woman patient I was asked to visit had just had surgery a month ago, but a wound was not healing properly so the doctor had ordered visiting nurses to start a new wound care for healing in the home.

Arriving, I found a pleasant, lovely white-haired woman who was still in bed in her pajamas. She was so tiny, maybe under 100 pounds. She had advised me I would find a key under the mat at the door and where I would find her bedroom. She lived with her daughter who was working. The home was very lovely and during our visit she informed me how she had raised her daughter on her own since the daughter was an infant. They have always lived together and were from a close-knit Italian family originally from upper New York State. Her daughter had a great job with an insurance company, so they moved to California together. She told me the whole story of an abusive husband, and she left him because she did not want her daughter growing up like that. Her daughter never married but found a great life and excellent career.

Her recent problems with her health involved having a malignant tumor removed from her stomach. The doctors felt they had gotten it all with no need for chemo or radiation. She was so sweet, in a great mood and wonderful attitude. I said, "You will be fine, and we will get your stomach wound healed."

I came to visit daily for a few weeks and the healing continued. She was gaining strength and informed the doctor of great progress!

Visits were decreased and I would be back in one week to check and do a protime blood test for coagulation because she was on blood thinners, which was common for her condition and history of a heart condition of atrial fibrillation.

I called early in the morning and she told me she was excited because she was going out for a drive and lunch with a friend. I informed her she really was not supposed to go out because she had home health services, and she should be homebound. But I did understand she had been confined for a long time, but we would be releasing her very soon.

She said if I come by 11:00 a.m. that would be fine and then her friend would pick her up. As I rang the doorbell, I heard her rush to the front door. The door opened and she was dressed and had her little white tennis shoes on. She was so excited and full of life and energy. We decided to go to the kitchen to do her blood test for convenience so I could set up there more easily.

We sat at the kitchen table; she faced the living room and I had my back to the living room. Taking her vital signs, I noticed she was looking over my shoulder and seemed to be smiling at something or someone.

I asked, "Are you OK?"

She smiled and calmly said, "Look over there on the fireplace. Do you see the beautiful little blonde girl playing there by the fireplace?"

I was so surprised, and she was intently looking and was so pleased at what she saw. I saw nothing. But I was paying close attention to everything she was seeing and what she was telling me. The little girl never went away the whole time I was there and during our visit. Her behavior confused me. She had never shown any signs of dementia or hallucinating during all my other visits. Her friend came to the door, and she rushed behind me to grab her coat and lock the door as if nothing was wrong.

Driving away, I pondered what I had just seen and experienced. I made the decision to call her doctor to inform him of the situation. I knew it would be hard to explain but felt I should at least report it to him. Not surprising, once on the phone I explained to the doctor what I had seen and what she was seeing in the living room. I told him how she had gone out to lunch and was walking, talking, and vital signs good but just this strange event. He was not pleased to hear what I had to say— almost like I was nuts—and I could hear it in his voice.

I finally said, "Doctor, I think your patient had her foot in the beyond!"

He went ballistic. "I saw her yesterday and she is perfect! I don't know what you are talking about."

"I just wanted to inform you. Thank you, goodbye."

She died unexpectedly the next day to everyone's surprise except mine!

22

The Mysterious

LIFE WITHOUT HER LEG

On a cold morning my nursing office sent me out to see one patient in the inner city who had recently had a vein transplant in her left leg. I was to check on the blood flow and make sure there were no problems.

Arriving in the Hispanic part of the city, I came to the house. It was an old charming craftsman, two stories and probably well over 100 years old. I love these old neighborhoods with history you can sense in the air and the big old mama trees that are always welcoming. I always sat in my car and centered myself in prayer before I went into an unknown house. I was there to serve and render the best service I could. I was at a time in my career of nursing where I also knew how important words were in the healing process. These words are at times more important than medicine. This has been seen over forty years of working with the sick.

I knocked on the sweet carved wooden door with a small stained-glass window at the top. Unable to see but only a shadow of a figure coming near to answer, I took a deep breath and sensed my feet to ground me. My patient's niece, a lovely young woman in her twenties, opened the door. She introduced herself and took me into the living room where her aunt, Mrs. T., was, I saw a very pale, slight woman with a bright spirit, very friendly and glad to see me. Inviting me in, I settled next to her and explained that I would take all her vital signs and then check the incisions on the left leg for healing and circulation. She was happy and agreed.

I checked all her vital signs, which were stable, and she had no fever. I was concerned about the color of her skin, a dark paleness, and as I moved down to observe her leg and remove the bandages, this leg did not look good. It was even more ashen than the rest of her and the pulses that needed to be there were missing, especially on her foot and pedal pulses. This was a huge surgery she had gone through to save her leg before. I had now gone into a deeper internal prayer. I did not want to tell her what I was seeing. As I was checking her leg, she started to share with me about her faith (she was Catholic) and I told her that I am a Christian. She shared about having dreams of her dead family members and even had negative thoughts of dying! I was trying to deal with all this and what was before me plus ongoing internal prayer. "If you want to live, you must not believe those voices and turn to prayer and your Savior the Christ."

She looked at me shocked. "OK."

I told her I would be back and had to go to my car for something. I went to my car and started to pray and ask what I should do. I saw no blood flow, felt no warmth in the newly operated leg. I felt so defeated, and now I must tell her or call the doctor's office. I finally got my answer to call the office. I called and informed them of my findings, and they said she was to go to hospital immediately.

Beyond sad, I went back and asked to see her niece, to have her there and inform them that she needed to go immediately to hospital and the ER to be checked. I only said I had concerns and the doctor agreed. Off she went, and I went on my way to see other patients, but the pain, hurt, and concern was almost unbearable!

I never forgot this patient and always had a sadness in my heart for her and her family. I rarely went into that part of the city, but when I did, I would always say a prayer as I passed by. I always wondered if she made it or was in heaven with her relatives. For over two years I had concerns but not the courage to stop by or call the doctor's office to ask whether she lived or died.

Then at the end of the two years I was in that part of the city and had the courage to stop! I knocked on the door and a young gentleman I didn't know answered the door. I asked for Mrs. T. with great hesitation and introduced myself as her former nurse.

He stared for a moment and then said, "Oh, she's at the casino having a grand time! She did lose her leg, but it doesn't keep her from living her best life!"

I said thank you and left feeling such great joy that she did overcome!

23

The Mysterious

SHARKS BELOW

My office informed me that today one of my patients was a World War II veteran, and I was to check on him after a hospitalization from gall bladder surgery. He was in his late eighties and was living with his wheelchair-bound wife. Sounded like a simple routine home visit and I would be in and out. But little did I know it would be far from routine!

Arriving in the nice middle-class neighborhood, I prepared myself as usual and then knocked on the door. A pleasant man in his eighties slowly opened the door. He was a very strong looking man for his age. The distinct features of his handsome youth were still there. I introduced myself and informed him of my routine to check his vital signs and ask him a few questions. His wife, I would say in her late seventies, rolled into the room in a wheelchair. She, too, was friendly and grateful to have me come to check on her husband. She said she was going back to her room and to make myself comfortable in the living room. You must understand that you are a stranger coming into their home and you start asking very personal questions. This is usually accepted, but with some people you could feel the tension. I was pretty good at making people feel comfortable and had the ability to make them feel vulnerable so they might open themselves to me about their life. Most nurses really care about the patient and give them a good amount of time to express themselves. This was one reason I really loved home care nursing, because I could manage my time more easily and some patients needed more time than others.

After I took his vital signs, he started sharing with me his concerns of his crippled wife and about her care. Not so much himself but real concern about who could care for her if something should happen to him. He married her when in his thirties, and when they met, she was already in a wheelchair, having been born with atrophic lower extremities. As he opened up about his concerns, I turned back to him and his health and concerns. He then started to share with me his experience as a young gunner in a plane during World War II. First, he took me down the hall and proudly showed me pictures of the plane he flew during the war. Now he was really excited to share more with me and began his amazing story, which was so hard to believe of an eighteen-year-old soldier.

He was the gunner in the bubble on the backside and bottom of the plane. The captain and pilot of the plane was only twenty-one years old. It was hard to imagine that, but these were our young men sent off to war. Babies really!

As he got more emotional and continued his story, I knew I would be there for a good while. My true soldier explained how they were flying over open water supposed to be inhabited by Japanese submarines. No US ships were to be in the area at all. J., stationed in his clear bubble, had a bird's eye view of the water, but even then, it was very difficult to make out any movement due to the rough seas. He told me he would have radio contact with the captain and one or two other crew members.

So, on this mostly clear day he was being very vigilant and looking closely for any submarines. It was difficult to stay so hyper alert, but it was war and a huge responsibility for such a young man. Suddenly he thought he saw something bobbing in the water. It was very tiny but the only reason he could see it was because it appeared to have an orange color around it! He informed the captain and the captain immediately radioed his commander and asked if a ship had been hit in that area, either US or Japanese? They said no American ships to their knowledge and to ignore and continue their mission. Now J. was seeing more orange bobbing objects, many more! He excitedly informed the captain. Again, the captain informed the commander and was told to ignore and carry on. He said it must be Japanese and to just leave the area!

J. was beside himself now believing this was human life floating, waving desperately in the middle of a vast ocean! J. yelled, "We need help and support! Those are human beings down there! Send a ship to rescue!" Again, the young captain was told to move out of the area. Now here is the most incredible part of the story! This young captain felt in his heart the commander was wrong. All on board the plane agreed with the captain. Against orders, the captain turned the plane around and went in lower and closer to the now obvious men floating in the rough sea.

"Men alive in the sea, hundreds of men alive!" J. yelled back to the captain.

The captain went over the head of the commander and alerted a nearby American ship to come in for the rescue, not knowing whether they were Japanese or American soldiers.

Now at this point in his story, J. began to sob. It took everything inside me not to join along with him. I went over and held him in my arms and let him cry. This soldier was crying for a young boy eighteen years old in a horrid war of man! My eyes filled with tears for him and for the amazing humanity of the young captain and his young crew to do the right thing despite the consequences! They really lived their truth. Always do the right thing and according to your heart and conscience.

J. informed me a movie had been made with Nicolas Cage called *USS Indianapolis, Men of Courage*. It is the true story of this ship on a secret mission carrying a nuclear warhead that had just been dropped off in the Soloman Islands. Over 1,195 young men, eighteen and nineteen years old were aboard. They were torpedoed by a Japanese submarine. Around 870 made it into the water. Many were eaten by sharks or died of starvation and the elements. No one was to know about this ship and the captain on the plane was told there were no US ships in the area. These were shark-infested waters full of our soldiers! I believe over 317 young men were saved because of the courage of these young men doing their godly, soul-connected duty to listen to their heart and mind connection. Beyond amazing, and this man touched my heart for the rest of my life! I was so honored to allow him to cry in front of me. I believe most of his tears were shed in private!

24

The Mysterious

A SIX-MONTH CONTRACT CHECKING ON DISABLED CHILDREN

While in L.A. I was working so hard and had seen so much I felt I really needed a break from home-health nursing and a change of pace. My prayer was answered in one week. A friend called and asked if I wanted to take a six-month government contract to check on disabled children and adults. The job required very little paperwork, and I would get to drive to private homes and facilities housing the disabled. Sounded like a great plan for change, less paperwork, and more money, plus better hours. I was in! Little did I know what I was getting myself into.

My first assignment was in beautiful Malibu Canyon, and I had to be there very early because I was to weigh all the residents before their breakfast. That meant around 7:00 a.m. I had to be good to go! Driving that lovely canyon before sunrise was great, and I was so elated to be on a new adventure. A great sense of calm came over me. After a nice long journey into the canyon my directions showed I needed to turn off into a smaller canyon. Remember no GPS in those days, no Google maps, just hand notes. The sun was now shining, so I could see much easier. This new canyon was full of eucalyptus trees and with the window down the smell permeated my nostrils.

Looking all around seeing only trees and creeks filled with water, I started to get nervous that I would not be on time and would not find this place in the wilderness. Then down the road a short distance and looking beyond the creek, I saw what looked like a small person in a bright colored tee shirt, waving their arms. Suddenly I saw a dirt road leading to a small, paved area toward a bridge to get to the other side. The person waving was yelling something but I could not make it out, so I rolled down my window as I parked in a car space. As I got out, I heard him so excited and he was yelling, "Welcome to God's country"! He was right! This was so beautiful, and he was my precious greeter. I could now see he was a young man with a disability, but he was so joyful and beyond the best welcome committee I ever saw. I was so thrilled to be there and to tackle my new adventure with these young people.

Now suddenly I was being greeted by twenty to thirty young and older disabled people. They all surrounded me and touched me in their excitement to have a visitor and mostly to be seeing a nurse. They knew I was not there to give them shots and had been informed by their counselors I would be seeing each one of them individually to weigh them and take their height and ask a few questions. Most were so happy to just have the individual attention. This would be an all-day event and take me into dinner time because of the numbers. I did get a few breaks and lunch breaks. While waiting for a patient I would get into their file and read up on their history. Some of them had been at this facility since it opened almost twenty to thirty years ago.

Some were younger and newer arrivals. As I read their charts, I could see many were born with birth defects but some, to my great concern, were disabled from either an overdose of penicillin or the sad statistic of vaccinations reactions. As we all know, we must make that decision for our own children, and we hope and pray our children will come out on top. But obviously some do not.

Working all day in this lovely environment with such heartfelt beautiful people including the staff was a wonderful experience.

I had a sweet office like a log cabin. All the doors and windows were open with a cool breeze moving all the time. I will not discuss all my friendly folks but want to share my time with my sweet greeter, Sam. He was around my age, which at the time was about forty-eight. He was short in stature with soft brown eyes, short arms and legs and a stout body with a protruding tummy. Very adorable actually!

When it was his turn to come and see me, I could tell he was very happy but nervous. I might say he stayed around earlier and took peeks around the corner while I was working.

I measured his height and weight. Then checked his vital signs, talking to him the whole time and asking him questions about his life and how he liked living in "God's country."

"I love my life and living here in God's country."

It is a very special place for special people and I absolutely agree.

This was another fabulous adventure. Restoring me with rest and change being able to see many more aspects of our world. An amazing gift of the special people I get to have a part of it!

25

Strange Encounters

THE BLUE NAIL POLISH OPENS HIS EYES

After moving to Kansas City and starting to work as a visiting home health nurse, my first assignment was in the inner city. Primarily in the black community. I had asked my supervisor if she thought it was a safe place and she said that none of the nurses had any problems. Being new to Kansas City from California, I was green as to working this area. Not stupid of inner-city work, I was aware and had some concerns.

In L.A. I had worked at a clinic in the inner city for the poor and indigent. After asking the supervisor and going out into the city I was very cautious.

The patient I am going to share with you was a forty-year-old quadriplegic who had been in a car accident and been basically bedbound for several years, only occasionally getting into a wheelchair according to my computer report. All the neighborhoods were very old pleasant-looking homes. Most were large and many family members lived together. Lovely trees lined the streets. So even though they were old and some in disrepair, the community was pleasing to look at and had a nice homey feeling.

DAILY MIRACLES AND ENCOUNTERS

As I parked on the street in front of the house, a relative was waiting for me. Friendly and nice the young man showed me the way down a dark hallway towards L.'s room. Nice old creaky wood floors and an overall comfortable feeling being in the home. Arriving at the patient's bedroom entrance, I was left alone with this young gentleman. He was in a hospital bed with what we call a special air mattress that is always inflating and deflating to help the immobile body to relieve pressure so sores will not form. I was so surprised how small and frail he was. This was from years of poor mobility and his overall nutrition. L. had his eyes closed tight, and as I introduced myself, he did not open his them. I could see movement under his lids as I spoke knowing that he knew I was there, and he was not asleep. This was somewhat a strange encounter. I never had a patient do this before even if they did not like nurses coming to their home.

It is difficult because nurses must get very personal and ask very private questions right away. I tried to be as kind and personable as possible because I was there to do some very personal tasks. I explained that I needed to take his vital signs and it was important for him to answer my questions. Not one word, nor would he open his eyes. I had years of experience, but I was feeling a little nervous because I was also there to turn him over and look at his back side. The family was concerned that his skin was starting to break down. Besides pressure and not being able to move, his nutrition played a huge part in his skin breakdown. We would get blood tests from the doctor to measure the protein albumin in the blood to help us determine what he needed, besides having a daily treatment plan for his wound care. Usually, we discuss with the doctors and make suggestions and get orders to move ahead and the nurse will come for several weeks to establish good care and healing and then we would teach the family members or relative who is willing to learn the treatment. L.'s main caregiver was his elderly mother in her late seventies.

I continued to talk and explain to him the importance of him answering me and opening his eyes. Nope, no chance! The window was open, and a nice breeze blew through the room. I got a great idea out of the blue. "Well, it makes me sad that you are not going to open your eyes and see my lovely blue nail polish I just got."

He slowly tried to squint and slightly open his eyes. I watched and he saw and quickly closed them again. "I guess you don't want to see fun heavenly things like my blue nail polish and the beautiful blue sky outside with the breeze blowing through your sheer white drapes. I wonder if you even believe in heaven."

He completely opened his eyes and said in a soft voice, "I do believe in heaven!"

We had now become friends, and he trusted me to open his eyes and allow me in. At that moment one of his brothers, about 6' 2" with no shirt on, tall, dark, handsome, and very intimidating, walked into the room and said in a loud voice, "Is everything good here, brother?"

L. replied, "All is good, brother."

He turned and walked away, and I was able to speak, touch, and comfort L., being compassionate and caring. I discussed the plan for his sores and care with a positive attitude and some humor and allowed the loving care to flow between us. All of this for me not giving up, pausing for a moment, and allowing the moment to reveal a simple act to challenge this young man to decide to open his eyes and see the blue nail polish. I will always remember him at that moment.

26

The Mysterious

A Dream of an Old Friend from High School

I had this dream while living in Kansas of an old friend from high school. There was a group of us who were very close. My sister and her boyfriend were a part of that group, and T. was a close friend of theirs. I was a few years younger but was allowed to hang out. I think they were around fifteen or sixteen years old, and I was maybe fourteen. Anyway, it was a very fun and exciting time! Especially because it was a big deal to be able to hang around with the older crowd. I never really dated T.. He was like a big brother along with my sister's boyfriend whom I called Big G.

There was a strong mutual respect and bond with all of us, and I suppose as a young girl I really looked up to T., my sister, and Big G. We would all go on cruises, meet at outside drive-ins and talk, drink soda, and just have fun. Like any teen having the freedom to go in a car, it was very exciting. A fun way of socializing.

We all lived in the beach area or close by. My sister and I were in San Clemente, California. T. and G. were from San Juan Capistrano. We all went to Capistrano

High School. This was a beautiful little town and community. The Old Mission of San Juan Capistrano was there, and my sister and I had gone to school for eight years at the Catholic grammar and middle school, under the oversight and run by very strict Maryknoll nuns.

As time went on in high school, we remained good friends. My sister married G., and T. started dating a friend of mine in our senior year. For me I was dating and serious about a young man from Newport Beach.

The picture was set! All young and close friends. Then after I married at the age of nineteen, I lost contact with T. I only heard stories about his life, his success in marriage, and with his business through my sister and her spouse.

Many years went by. I divorced and remarried. Many years passed and my husband and I moved to Kansas City. By now it had been maybe forty-five years since I had seen or spoken to T. Then one night I had a vivid dream about him and that he was not doing well. At that time of my life, I was working at the Kansas City Holistic Center. I worked with patients and clients all over the country. From cancer patients and many other multiple problems. We had many alternative treatment plans and suggestions to help restore people back on track to health.

In the dream we were just talking as friends, and he was telling me he did not understand why he was so ill because he was still pretty young. I felt this instant compassion and was listening intently to his every word. My heart like a sister went out to him with genuine concern!

Then suddenly the dream was over. I woke up and this concern and feeling would not go away. As soon as I could, I got on the phone to my sister's ex-husband and told him about my dream. It all seemed very real, and I could not let it go. He was shocked as he listened to me and said I was right. T. was very ill with many problems. I asked him to please call him and tell him to call me. I might be able to help in some way.

T. called me at work the very next day, and we were able to share about his illness, marriage to my friend, and many wonderful memories. I was able to give him some suggestions for an alternative medicine, and he was forever grateful and more than anything pleased with the warm, loving sister connection. The Love Connection! The most important connection of all. I expressed my love for him and to send my love to his wife, my friend.

I received a call several months later that T. had passed. He was so young really and such a jewel of a human being. I tried very had to go to the funeral in San Clemente but was unable to book a flight to go and give my condolences which had to be by phone. But I also knew we had a higher connection that the Higher gave us! An amazing miracle really. It makes me realize the importance of the Love Chain Connection!

27

The Mysterious

YOU NEED TO FIND GOD

My journey my search, for truth and a connection with the Higher or God started early on in my twenties. I had married very young at nineteen and had my first child by the age of twenty-two. Like most young people, I was idealistic and thought I knew what I wanted and what marriage was all about! Well, I did want a marriage and family but had no idea what I was stepping into. I just knew in my soul I thought I could do a much better job at it than my parents had done. First of all, in my observation they always fought about money. So, I would marry someone who had a good idea of making money, was educated, and came from a good family, which I did. All looked great on the outside. People always said we looked like the perfect couple, almost like a prince and princess. We had a huge, lovely wedding and a honeymoon to Hawaii. Everything was going as the dream should. Well not quite!

On our way back from our honeymoon there was an air strike and very few planes flying. This was in 1966. We were on a United Airlines flight to come home but got stranded for many hours at the Kauai airport then at

Oahu with very little food or snacks available. When we finally boarded the plane, we were beyond exhausted. In those days, you a fully prepared meal was served once the plane was in the air. So, we knew relief was in sight.

Once the plane was in the air and everyone settled in, the stewardess started to serve our dinner trays. At this point we were beyond excited to have food. The tray was served and there were two lovely meals all hot and steamy. We both started to eat and I occasionally paused and looked out the window, thinking and contemplating my new life now and what was ahead of me.

As I turned back to finish my meal, I realized nothing was left! My husband had devoured my dinner without saying a word! I stared in shock, not believing what had happened. I may not have even said anything because I was so upset and shocked. This was my new husband and the person I was now starting a new life with. I took a deep breath and felt the pain and turned my head back to look out the window. It was then I knew I had made a huge mistake in my life. I just knew!

I did love this man as much as a person can I suppose. I was willing to give it a real good shot. We had so much going for us and decent money. He was a young page at NBC studios, working his way up to becoming a director. We had two nice cars and a lovely house in Northridge, California. We were on our way to starting a family and everything looked pretty darn good, except that gnawing feeling deep down and hidden in my gut. I think I made a bad mistake. Oh! I had no idea what I had stepped into. Remember this was the sixties. Things were crazy. Sex, hippies, and rock and roll. Well, we were conservative in our views. Love, family, and stability. Occasionally went to church but we were drifting from that now that we were on our own. The problems that raised their heads were not the home situation; it was his work environment. He was doing shows at NBC with the Mamas and the Papas, Diana Ross and the Supremes, the Beatles, and the Johnny Carson Show! I would often get the chance to attend these shows and it was very exciting at first.

After our first child came, it was not much fun or interesting to go anymore. That's when change came, and I and my child basically became abandoned! He was never home. Fourteen to sixteen-hour days! I had no idea what I had stepped into.

All the money, clothes, big house, cars but nothing except complete loneliness and sadness. My daughter and I only had each other. My whole family and friends were down on the coast and so we would go on the weekends for comfort.

This intense loneliness is what really started me on my search for truth and a deeper spiritual meaning in my life. My friend gave me a Bible and I began the task of reading Revelation. I still to this day do not know why but I was determined to understand something on my own through this difficult read. I did experience a great change and had an epiphany after reading it. This started the complete change in my life.

So, during this time my daughter was about ten months old, and I needed a break. I got a babysitter two days a week and took a job in Beverly Hills at a well-known beauty salon called Gene Shacove's on Rodeo Drive in Beverly Hills, California.

I was hired as a makeup artist in the front of the salon. Many stars would come in on a daily basis, and there were lots of hairdressers from all over the world. They all wanted to work there.

This was a great time for me and I was only away from my baby girl for a few days a week.

At my station in front of the main desk, I would watch and see all the stars come and go for their appointments and wait on my appointments. I would keep to myself and would sit and read my Bible.

I noticed a lot of the hairdressers would come in loaded, with their colored sunglasses on in the early part of the day, and they were not very happy or friendly until much later in the day. This was understood, it was the sixties. The owner, Gene, was always very late for his appointments and would have people sitting, lined up, coming out of his private room which was near my station.

People would be mad but said he was worth the wait, even if they had flown into California from another state to get their hair cut. He would rush in with colored glasses and a fur coat on in December and a leather bag over his shoulder. He would rush right past me and never give me the light of day. But he had been the one who hired me for the job. At my job interview he had me pivot around him so he could check me out. I got hired, but I did resist his request saying I was a new young mother. He laughed!

These, as I said, were very exciting and scary times.

Remember this was during the time of the Manson murders and all those people were clients of Gene Shacove! Sharon Tate and all of them. While I was still working, there the whole salon went crazy with fear and everyone was paranoid. I was really nervous also, but I never did drugs, and I was reading my Bible which gave me great peace and conviction.

DAILY MIRACLES AND ENCOUNTERS

I did not want to quit my job, but the fear and paranoia was beyond tolerable. So, I gave notice I was leaving. My last day at the salon was a quiet day and I had just finished doing a customer's eyebrow trim, so I as always was sitting quietly and reading my Bible. As I was sitting and reading, one of the hairdressers approached me. I knew him and he was never very friendly, but I said hello. He was always very loaded on pot and was this day. He had on rose-colored glasses, was very thin, and I felt a great sadness about him. Everyone was fearful because the police still had not captured Charles Manson and his group who had committed six murders, so all these people were on edge because they sold dope.

This hairdresser was just standing weak and wobbling in front of me. "I want to know what makes you so peaceful? I want that kind of peace!"

I looked right into his eyes and said, "You need to find God in your life."

He stared at me in bewilderment. That was my last day, and I did not think I would ever see him again. But the Higher had another plan.

Ten years later during a very happy time in my life, I had a new marriage, new baby girl, and a growing faith. I was approached on the streets in the San Fernando Valley by a man who called out my name. I turned around and did not really recognize him. He reminded me of when we all worked together at Gene Shacove's and then I remembered.

"I want to thank you for changing my life," he said.

I looked at him shocked and said I did not understand.

"When I was so lost and scared you told me to find God in my life and I did. Thank you for helping change my life!"

28

Small Tales, Big Miracles

MOTHER'S DEATH

I was traveling from California with my husband to visit Kansas City (a few years before we moved). My elderly mother lived alone in Escondido, California. She was eighty-four years old and still very spry physically but losing some memory.

It was Mother's Day weekend, and we were flying back to see family (my daughter and grandchildren) plus my husband's sister was flying in from Florida to see her son. At the time there were quite a few family members living in KC. This is one reason we had been planning to move there one day.

My mother was very difficult and stubborn, but I was always able to keep close to her where my brother and sister were really estranged from her. I would not consider her the best mom. We spoke on the phone weekly, and I would visit her if she allowed it when I would go to San Diego to visit my daughter who was in college.

I had spoken to her several days before leaving to visit KC, which was a Friday. I was unable to reach her on the phone Friday morning but continued my trip with my spouse. I can truly say I had this unsettling feeling deep in my chest that something was wrong. Upon arriving in KC, I tried again many times and was unable to reach her. I knew something was wrong. I finally called the Escondido Wellness check line to have them check on her. I received the fateful call that they found my mother deceased on the floor next to the refrigerator. My greatest concern was now a reality! I lost my mother on Mother's Day weekend. I asked the day watchman to please cover her with a blanket, put a towel under her (she was lying in urine), lock the house up, and leave the keys under the door mat. I informed them I would call the San Diego Coroner's Office because my niece worked there as a mortician. She would handle all details and remove my mother's body to the coroner's office, and I would get on a plane as soon as possible and fly into San Diego from Kansas City.

After arriving, I went to my mother's home and my husband and I started going through all her papers. We hired an attorney to file probate. My mother had not done her will. She thought she had but it was actually my stepfather's who was now deceased, so it was null and void.

I had no time to grieve. My daughters flew in and helped. We were there over a week, had a funeral for her, and buried her in Escondido.

All of us locked up the house and flew to different parts of the country. Tony and I went back to Los Angeles. All of this took place in one week. I never could catch my breath or even think of a time to really grieve.

Once home, our house was all dark and closed. I walked down the hallway to my small office, turned on the lights and the grief really hit me hard. I called and cried out to my mother and God to show me a sign that my mother was OK.

Tears streamed down my face, and I went to sit at my computer to check my schedule. At that time, I was still working as a nurse. All the shades on my window were closed, so I went to open the window and shades near my desk. A year ago, I had planted a little Zen garden just outside my window, all with plant clippings from my mother's garden she had given me over time. The garden was always lovely and green but never flowered because it was in a shaded area. As I pulled back the shade and opened the window, the most beautiful fragrance filled my room. I was shocked and my eyes could not believe what was in front of me! The garden was in full bloom. Not only bright green plants but yellow, red, magenta, white, and lavender flowers, all blooming. This was really a miracle! My mother's' plants all in full bloom. The flowers lasted for an entire week and never bloomed again no matter how hard I tried to bring them back. The Lord and my mother let me know that "All is well!"

SMALL TALES
MY MOTHER - LOOK FOR THE DIAMOND RING

After several weeks of working with the attorney and a realtor we had to go back down to my mother's house and prepare for the estate and home to be sold.

I cannot express the pain and sorrow we have to endure when we lose a loved one!

Pulling up to her house again and seeing her Chevy station wagon parked in the driveway was beyond painful. This time was only myself and my husband going into the home. We moved around the house and did all we could to prepare for the upcoming estate sale. Other family members and I had already gone through the personal things like pictures and small items that reminded us of her and taken home what we wanted. Everything left would be part of the estate sale. We hired a company to do the work, therefore, we would not even be present.

I walked around in silence, being connected to myself and allowing the grief to be and move through me. We were getting ready to lock up the house forever, leaving all that remained of my mom's things. Just leave!

My husband, Tony, was in front of me and walking out the front door. He turned and said, "Are you coming?"

"Yes," I responded with a very heavy heart. As I was leaving, suddenly I heard very clearly in my head, "Go get the diamond upstairs." I stopped in my tracks. I had just been upstairs and gone through everything, even her shoes where I found $50 cash. But this was not to be ignored. So, I ran back upstairs and looked on the bed where hundreds of pictures and bags of old-fashioned gloves and jewelry still sat on the master bed. I was instinctively shown to go to the bag of gloves. There were about ten pair all rolled over in pairs. As I reached my hand, I started squeezing and sure enough inside a pair of dark purple gloves was a small dark blue velvet box and inside was a beautiful diamond ring my mother wanted me to keep from the estate sale!

29

Small Tales, Big Miracles

ET Murphy from Above

While working in Los Angeles as a visiting nurse, I was given an assignment to see a woman who had been in a terrible car accident way back in the 1940s. She had been in her twenties then and wheelchair bound as a paraplegic since the accident. She was now in her nineties and had been bedbound for several years and had developed bad bed sores.

Her history was fascinating, and I was really interested in learning and hearing the full story of how she got where she was! I was also interested in her treatment plan from the doctor. We would clean the wounds, and then pack them with manuka honey and sugar before covering them with bandages. This was all new to me, but I had been reading up on this as a great new way to heal wounds. As a holistic nurse, I was all-in to try a natural cure.

Slowly driving up the Sherman Oaks hill I was up high looking over the entire San Fernando Valley, and it was such a lovely clear day. The air was clean, and I suddenly had this heavenly thought. *This is the perfect name for this patient! ET!* Extraterrestrial living high on the mountain.

As I approached the lovely cottage set up high on the mountain, I had the most calming feeling yet so excited to see what ET would be like and to hear her story. This was really one of the great gifts as a nurse to hear the patients' stories.

The house was lovely and probably built in the 1940s or '50s. Cozy and quaint, surrounded by soft green trees cascading all around.

After parking and strolling up the front doorsteps I thought to myself, *Wow! If this patient is wheelchair and bedbound, someone will have to carry her to get her into the car or get around anywhere on the property.* I would soon have my questions answered. Close to the front door I noticed again the beautiful landscape, smell of flowers, the gentle breeze against my face and off to the side an elderly man with a straw hat working in the garden. I was thinking perhaps it was just a friend helping ET.

I rang the doorbell. A lovely lady answered and invited me in. She introduced herself as the personal assistant and homemaker for ET. Entering the room there was such a feeling of calmness. And this cozy home had floor to ceiling windows both in the front and back of the home, showing rolling hills and gardens brimming with flowers. Hanging in the back were three to four hummingbird feeders, and there were so many birds feeding, their multiple colors glistening in the sun! Wow! So far this had been a magical experience.

The caregiver showed me the way to my patient and announced my name. Sitting in a king-sized bed was this most adorable human being who really did look like she was from another planet! E.T was such a perfect name for her. She sat smiling at me with her fluffy snow hair and huge thick coke bottle glasses. The smile was very warm and welcoming even though I know she was struggling a lot with her situation and poor healing bed sores.

I looked around this grand bedroom, which was unpretentious. But the bedroom had glass on two sides, and she had a full view of the Valley and the garden on the other side. Though she had been through a lot, her environment was magical, and I was sure she helped to create this for herself!

We hit it off right away as she had me pull up a silky pink boudoir chair. When I am meeting a patient for the first time I take as much time as possible to get familiar and build their trust before doing very intimate procedures. I always had a sensitivity to the needs of my patients and showed them I genuinely cared about their wellbeing. I was in their home and on their territory.

As we started to talk, I asked how she ended up in a wheelchair and what happened with her car accident back in the forties.

She was a real spitfire in her twenties, working as a buyer for a huge department store. She was confident, carefree, and had a fiancé and a red sports car. She had gotten a call from her boss that she needed to go to San Francisco to do some buying for the store.

She was so excited about her new red sports car she decided to drive up the coast. Can you imagine what the roads were like in the 1940s? Oh my gosh! All her friends and fiancé begged her not to go, but she went anyway. She drove US Route 101 and Highway 1 all the way up the coast of California. So scary to think she would do this all alone in a little convertible sports car.

She showed such excitement and animation of her

arms as she went into the details of her great adventure in her newly purchased car. Driving up the coast on a clear beautiful day, not a cloud in the sky, she left L.A. and headed up the coast towards San Francisco. She had packed her suitcase, tied it to the trunk, made herself some sandwiches, and told everyone *adios, amigos*!

The day was going great. She felt on top of the world and was now going up on Highway 1 beyond Big Sur. Not a care in the world and no other cars or a person insight. Suddenly, a huge bumble bee started to buzz around her head. She started to swat at it but it was not going away! She didn't want to stop on this bad two-lane highway alone. So, one last swat and she suddenly lost control of the car. She went over a one-hundred-foot cliff on a desolate beach with no one in sight or nearby. Her car became lodged in a tree, the front end facing the ground. She was badly injured and hanging halfway out of the car, her head down and her extremities stuck in the wreckage. She said she was unconscious for a while then woke up screaming for help, then finally stopped because she knew no one would hear her or help her. Being a believer, she surrendered her fate to the Divine and waited to die. She hung there for several days, but by Divine intervention a man was walking his cow on the beach and found her almost lifeless body. She was eventually rescued, but can you imagine how long it took? No cells phone then and out in the middle of nowhere, but through His grace she survived.

Not only did she survive but she never let her paralyzed legs keep her down. She became a writer for many news articles and many magazines. She bought her dream home and did not let others try to talk her out of it!

She has had a marvelous life and never felt sorry for herself. Her finance did break off the engagement after her accident, and she never married or had children, but he came crawling back after a few years. They did get married and he has taken care of her, carried her to the car and all around with and without her wheelchair all these years! By the way, the elderly little man in the garden with the straw hat, Mr. ET!

30

Small Tales, Big Miracles

"AM I A MAN OR A WOMAN?"

I was coming to the close of my working day around 5:00 p.m. in L.A. when I got a call from my office saying they had an emergency and would I please go see this patient who had just gotten out of the hospital and was living in a hotel room. He'd had surgery for a gall bladder removal and needed all his vital signs and dressings checked. With hesitation I accepted the patient even though I was really exhausted, and it was getting dark.

Upon arriving at his room, I was taken aback when he opened the door. I had a strange sensation and impression of him. He felt to me kind of like a she! I introduced myself as his nurse and he invited me in and was very friendly and warm. As we sat and I shared I would check his incision and take his vital signs, he continued to share with me about his life. Soon he was very comfortable with me and opened about his whole life story to his best ability and it started like this. He was an engineer for a large rocket company in L.A. and had been married with two grown children. He always struggled with his identity of being a male or a female. Now this was back in the 1990s; talk like this was not seen much or discussed.

As a nurse we have some knowledge, but this was pretty new in my own experience. I sat very attentively because he was now confirming what I had instinctively felt when I came to the door. Not only was he transitioning to be female, but he had been living in a camper to save money to help pay for his divorce and children's college.

He had to stay at the hotel because he was having surgery. I sat very attentively listening to his story and trying to be open and not judge. And as I listened more deeply, I had this great sense of compassion come over me. This was a very good person and a new exchange for me. I tried very hard to set myself aside and listen.

Continuing, he had started to transition into a woman having hormone therapy. This was very difficult with the hormones and very scary. He could lose his job, which would be horrid for his children and their college. At one level, this was unbelievable to me. I thought someone had to be *really* suffering to go through all this, and he was still hurting so badly. He continued to share, almost being grateful that I was willing to listen to him without judgement. He had a clear slate with me because I had no opinion at this time and very little knowledge of his situation. Then as if I could not believe what he was saying the story got more intense! Like people say this could not have been made up in a movie. Life is more exciting and riveting than any movie.

He said that while going through all this hell and transition starting the female hormone treatment and all, he found someone and fell in love. No not with a man but with a woman! He met his real soul mate so now was slowly going back to being a male. Oh my gosh! Compassion poured over me and I reached out to give him a hug.

He began to weep in my arms and said that through all this torture he had never given up in his search for and love of the Lord.

Now I was in a state of love and compassion all at the same time. He said, "The Lord must love me so much that he sent a woman to love me wholly for who I am. I never gave up on the love of the living Christ to help me through this maze of hell. Even when I was not listening and so confused. I never gave up the search for that Love. Now He sent a woman to prove that He really loves me!"

31

Small Tales, Big Miracles

"I WILL COME VISIT YOU WHEN I DIE."

Working in the early 1980's at a large hospital in L.A., I was very eager and excited to help and learn all I could about life and people. I was an ICU/CCU nurse (intensive care and coronary care). These were the places to work to have excitement and see your skills work at hand to those in real need.

After being at that hospital for about a year, I was comfortable with it and the staff that I worked closely with. It was almost like a sisterhood because there were very few male nurses. But of course, when we did have the privilege of a male nurse, we loved it because he had lifting skills and strength when we needed his help.

I liked working the 3:00 to 11:00 p.m. shift because most doctors had left, and it was quieter and calmer during the evening shift. I received my patients for the night, which was never more than two because they had your undivided attention. That was another reason I wanted to work the ICU/CCU units. It was doable, not like being on a regular floor where you would get fifteen to eighteen patients. That was almost impossible to give good nursing care. So, I loved my shifts in ICU/CCU. I could give my patients the best care.

One night on duty, I went to introduce myself to my patients, even if they were on a ventilator. That night I had one patient on a vent and the other was not.

My second patient was a middle-aged woman, very pale but with a lovely smile and great attitude despite of her situation. As we exchanged and got to know each other during the evening shift, she shared with me that she, too, was a nurse. Of course, that really opened the door for us to share and exchange with each other like sisters.

I was aware of her diagnosis of terminal cancer, and she shared with me that she knew her time to go was soon. She was not fearful and was looking forward to it as a great adventure! She was really a breath of fresh air even during this very sad and difficult time in her life. Coming to grips with that, this was the end of her life.

As we talked and she shared her thoughts about her next adventure, she said to me, "When I die, I will come and visit you and let you know that I am OK."

Being a young naive nurse, I said, "OK." It just felt natural, and we had a deep connection.

I had not worked in the ICU for a week and was home talking in the hallway with my teenage daughter. As we were talking, the light in her bedroom went out suddenly. She reached over and turned it back on. We continued to talk in the hall, and it happened again. My daughter screamed and said, "There is a ghost in there!"

"Go into the living room. I know who it is, one of my patients!"

I just knew it was Merriam! I went into the room, closed the door, and I could feel her presence in the room. I spoke with her. "I know it is you, Merriam, and I appreciate your promise to let me know you are on your way to your heavenly place but you are really scaring my teen daughter. I will pray with you and for you to be on your way! Much love and kisses!"

Suddenly I no longer felt her in the room. I assured my daughter all was clear, but she slept in our room for a few nights to make sure.

As I pondered the experience, I came to realize that the front room was my husband's and mine for a long time. We had just changed rooms with our daughter to let her have more room.

Truly, we are spiritual beings on this earth for a short time.

Strange Encounters
OPPRESSIVE BLACK BURKAS

Working in Kansas City I had learned to really be aware of the huge amount of missionary and non-profit work done by many churches and organizations. It was quite impressive. Also, the work in the inner city and with the poor through Catholic Charities. Many of my patients, both in Missouri and Kansas, received a huge amount of help and funding.

I learned to appreciate the large gala parties of the rich for non-profit organizations and the help given and received through generous giving. Along with this knowledge the suffering and lack that affects the poor and sick during times of strife and recession which we felt hard hit during the 2008 recession.

I met missionaries from Kansas who had come back in town maybe due to an illness or having a baby. They always amazed me with their work and calling, and most were eager to go back to Africa or the Third World countries they ministered in. Amazing work really and so real.

While in Kansas working, I got a call from my office explaining that this woman in Olathe needed to be seen but she did not speak a word of English and all communication had to be through her son. I was given his number. He was warm and friendly and I was invited to come to the home. It was later in the day, and they would be my last stop of the day.

The home was a cute split-level in a nice neighborhood . I knocked on the door. The son, in his fifties, came to the door and welcomed me in.

As I was led up the stairs to the next level, the stairway had a metal railing that opened to the living room. I looked to my left into the living room and there were four middle-aged women and one elderly woman sitting quietly on the sofa. All were dressed in black burka's covering their entire bodies and faces. It was a hot summer day and even with air conditioning it was very hot!

They all stared at me through their veils. The eyes of each one piercing and fearful! My first impression was of oppression, almost like a feeling of tightness around my neck. I have friends that are Islamic, and I have read a little of the Quran, and I knew this was not right. I went deeper into myself and connected with myself with a deep prayer and tried not to judge. But it felt so unjust to my free godly spirit. Compassion came over me, and I continued up the stairs. At the top of the stairs, the son called to his mother and introduced us to the best of his ability to translate and explained to her what the nurse was here to do. I was there to change her urinary catheter, which had been way beyond its changing time. I didn't know how long they had been in this country or if it was when she came from Afghanistan.

She was the warmest of all the women. The others just seemed so fearful, which was understandable. Foreign country, not speaking the language, and me doing very private personal body care to the elder mother. Not surprising to be in a fearful state! I had to rise above my fearful state.

The son walked us down the hall to a bedroom and closed the door. I tried to be very warm, comforting, and assuring with my gestures as I guided her to the bed to lay down. She lifted her face veil and showed her warm smiling face. She seemed to understand me.

You can only imagine the situation. We just met and she is so modest, and I was going to lift her robe and remove an old catheter in her urinary tract, clean her, and open a sterile kit with new catheter and insert it. Hopefully, with my years of skill, it would go into the right spot. Because if it didn't, I did not have another kit to replace it tonight. I lifted my eyes upward and prayed for guidance and help of the Divine.

Lifting her robe and upon examination of her private area, I was beyond shocked to see something I had never seen in my thirty-five years of nursing! Her body pubic hair was completely wrapped around the catheter a good three inches from the urinary opening down. My medical scissors would never work with their blunt ends. Oh Lord, I thought! This is beyond a nightmare. But how do I explain to her what I must do? I worked so hard to remain calm and gestured I would be right back. She seemed to understand. This impossible situation had now gotten more impossible. I had to go and explain to her son that I need sharp scissors. I did not go into detail because this was his mother and to honor their customs and his mother. The others just sat staring at me in horror, not really understanding what was happening to their elder.

I went back into the room, and she was smiling at me and still had her veil up so I could see her gentle face. I made the gestures the best I could of what I had to do and tried to reassure her. I felt she was comfortable with me and trusted me.

I gently started to carefully cut around the catheter and very close to her urinary opening. It felt like an eternity, but finally complete release, and I was able to remove, clean her, and put in new catheter.

As I carefully helped her up, she smiled, put her veil down, and we hugged each other warmly.

Then we walked out to let everyone in the room see that all was well.

The mood changed and the room felt lighter and not so oppressed and dark.

We are all human and can reach way beyond our norms and culture to love and honor each other.

Again, love and compassion win!

33

The Miraculous

CAR REPAIR - A SIGN!

It was an extremely hot day in the San Fernando Valley, like around 106 degrees even in the Malibu area where I was being sent to see a patient. I loved my little sports car, a fun-to-drive Mazda hatchback. But even with air conditioning going in and out of the car, it was rough.

On my way out of the Valley to Malibu I exited off Kanon Road to see my patient who lived off the grid. Coming off the exit, I noticed a large dump truck at the stop sign on a slight hill. He rolled back into my car and crunched the front end and then sped away not even knowing he did it! I pulled over and was so upset getting out and seeing the damage to the front end. Dented and the paint scraped off! This made me so sad, but I continued the drive to see my patient nearby.

After taking care of my patient, I was driving back into the Valley and as I was coming over the top of the hill, I had a conversation with the Lord. "I work so hard and need and love my car. I know it does not seem important, but I wish my car was not dented and I had the money to fix it." Then I let it go, not knowing about repairs, money, etc.

I pulled off the freeway and was going into a grocery store to get something to drink but first sat for a few minutes, catching my breath from the morning catastrophe. Sitting there with my eyes closed with the engine running and air on, I heard a tap on my window. Looking up I saw a nice younger man and I felt in a safe area to roll my window down.

"Hi! I can fix your car right here in the parking lot for $100 while you go into the grocery store?"

I looked into his eyes and I knew this was a gift!

Because of the prayer and just the place I was at I knew that I knew this was a gift. Most people would think this is crazy, but I was working at this time in another time zone. I trusted him, yes with a question of losing, but I went with it.

I went into the large store, walked around, and got a drink and something to eat while believing and excited to see what would happen. I thought at times, how can he fix my car so fast?

After about twenty minutes, I walked back to the parking lot. No one was near my car and, it being low I could not see if the damage had been fixed.

I got more and more excited and as I approached it was completely fixed and you could not even tell where the new paint was. The dent was fixed and painted! The man was gone and nowhere in sight for me to even thank him!

This was truly a day of perfect alignment and a simple prayer answered!

Strange Tales

HOMELESS MAN ON THE STREET - A MESSAGE

I was in the Valley working as a nurse but was having a difficult time because I was so exhausted and needed a break from it for a while. So, I took a job with a doctor friend's office to be his nurse and was also starting an attempt at a business working with children with my closest friend.

Not being business minded, I found this task difficult also but it was a nice break from taking care of the sick. I just needed a change of pace for a while and it seemed like a great idea to help youth.

As I pulled off the freeway on another very hot day in the Valley, I was frustrated about many things with my business adventure. I had a family with teens and the new job with the doctor.

Again, I felt almost angry at myself for taking on so much and did not know how to resolve the problems I was encountering at that time. I was so frustrated with myself and began talking to myself in my frustration. Tears spilled down my cheeks.

The freeway ramp was full of cars in Woodland Hills, forcing me to slow down. Ahead of me stood a man in the center cement divider holding a sign. I was thankful for the slowdown of traffic so I could compose myself.

As my car moved closer, he tapped on my window and looked right into my eyes. I slowly rolled the window down, not feeling at all fearful. I saw in his eyes that he was at more peace than I was, even though he was on the street asking for money to survive.

"Don't fret, dear sweet lady. Don't you know the Lord is always near you and hearing your voice?"

My whole state changed, and I let go. I was able to see clearly and make clear decisions from that day during these difficulties.

This again taught me to listen and be open as to where a good word or a gift of encouragement might come from. You cannot put the Divine in a box.

35

Strange Encounters
FIRST AIDS PATIENT IN 1982

There had been rumors in the hospital about a strange new disease going around among the gay population. In the 1980s gay people were much more covert in their relationships and did not have the rights that are now available. So, all the talk about this new disease was very hush hush even in the hospital. And of course, the fears involved were great also for everyone including the doctors and nurses. I always tried to be vigilant about what was going on around me and especially in the hospital and with patients.

During my prayer and meditation time I was, at times, able to foresee certain things about my patients or certain treatments would be revealed to me during this time. I had recently read a very tiny article in the *L.A. Times* about a strange new disease going around the gay population, confirming the rumors at the hospital. When I read this, I had a strong feeling in my solar plexus that this was going to be a big deal. And boy was I right!

Within one week of reading this article, I was working the 3–11 shift in ICU, and we gathered to receive our nightly report from the early shift to change hands and each nurse to get her two patient assignments. Because the patients are so sick, we would get only two each. As the morning nurse was giving a report on my patients, it dawned on me that this is one of those strange cases. Of course, we did not know if the gentleman was gay or not but it all did not add up during the report, and I put two and two together. The report was as if someone was really covering their tracks. I mean the doctor. It was well known that this one doctor had a reputation for taking care of gay patients and the patient had no health insurance (many did not during those days) and the patient just sounded way too sick to just have a diagnosis of pneumonia.

During the report I blurted out to all the nurses. "I think this is one of those strange new cases in the gay community. We had better be careful and use extra precautions!"

Everyone agreed and to wear masks, gloves, and extra gowns even though nothing had been ordered to indicate we needed these precautions.

The doctor was protecting the young man and did not want him to not receive the care he needed. It was not fair to the other doctor and nurses, but that is why you always have to be on your toes and pay close attention to what is happening.

This patient was well taken care of in ICU, and we stabilized him. But because of the condition and vast amount of care required, the doctors decided to have him transferred to a private room on a regular medical surgical floor and to be put in isolation. All the blood work was coming back. AIDS had already been seen in other countries and now the news was starting to flood all over. There was so much fear and misinformation about the disease and how contagious it was. But now we were hearing people were starting to die in large numbers in the gay community.

Back to my patient in ICU. When I came back to work for my shift the next day, I was asked to be a float nurse and go up and help take care of this patient that we now knew had full blown AIDS. I still had a teen child at home and my husband, but I felt strong enough in my skills as a nurse that I could do this and protect myself and my family. I was trained in isolation techniques, and I was informed I would have a chair outside his door and would not have to be inside the entire time.

I had to completely gear up each time I went in and throw all gear in an isolation bin every time I went out. This was like private duty nursing because it is impossible for any nurse to do this and have another ten to fifteen patients to take care of. The nurses on his floor were very grateful to have me there.

The truth of the matter was I hardly had a moment to sit and was in the room for long periods of time. He was very demanding, which was understandable. He was isolated, not allowed company, and a very sick young man. He had chronic oozing greenish diarrhea that burned like hell if it got on his skin. The first time, I went to clean him up in war gear. I had a head cover, face mask, face shield, gloves, double gown over a jump suit. All the paper gowns, masks, and pads under the patient were discarded each time I was in the room. I had to be very mindful and take care of business. Like I said, I was in the room for almost the whole eight-hour shift anyway because he was so needy and needed ongoing care.

Going into his room for the first time in my war gear I really felt sorry for him. Compassion poured over me as I introduced myself knowing he would not remember me from ICU. He did not.

I explained I was there to help him be comfortable, take his vital signs, and clean him up. I also made sure he had supplies of water, juice, and snacks if wanted in his room. He was in isolation with very little contact with the rest of the floor staff. I was his nurse for eight hours.

He was sedated but also seemed very disoriented, which we later learned was not uncommon with AIDS because it attaches to the brain cells. At that time, it was not known.

He was very open with me and talked while I was in the room. He never stopped talking! I did not mind because I had some daunting tasks in front of me.

As I informed him, I was going to clean up the diarrhea. I can remember a smell of death that I had never smelled before. As I cleaned away, I could see his rectum, which was a huge hole about the size of a grapefruit and completely ulcerated! *Oh, My Lord, have mercy!* He continued to share his personal experiences and almost bragging that he'd had almost 500 different sexual experiences and he was proud of it! The contrast of him telling me his stories of his one-night stands and his sexual fantasies was in such contrast to what I was seeing and what I had to do to help him be comfortable and show as much compassion during his last days on Planet Earth.

He died a terrible slow death all alone in a hospital isolation room with only the doctors and nurses as his friends and merciful companions until he took his last breath.

DAILY MIRACLES AND ENCOUNTERS

The AIDS epidemic, as most know, took a huge toll on many young and old lives, spreading all over the world. It took years of learning and research to finally gain some control with medications, sexual education, and many healthier choices that people had to learn to be able to live a longer life if following this lifestyle.

During those years and my whole nursing career of forty years I had many HIV patients and encounters in L.A. and Kansas City.

I have met many wonderful people in the gay community helping me to go way beyond myself and judgement and open my heart even more for compassion and love, to care for the sick and the suffering.

Unnerving

Darkness

One of the most difficult cases I have ever had to endure was in L.A. I took care of this patient and really her family for almost a year before I moved to Kansas. It was a heart-wrenching situation. A young mother in her forties had been in a terrible car accident several years prior, which left her paraplegic, only able to use her upper arms.

The story begins with her husband and two teen children driving in the mountains of Northern California in a camper for a nice summer vacation together. After her husband had driven several hours, she offered to drive. This is when tragedy struck! She was driving on a winding mountain road and a car came around the corner and made her swerve, tipping the top-heavy camper over and down a one-hundred-foot cliff. All the family were injured, but A. was stuck under the stirring wheel and unable to move her legs during the final rescue attempt to remove everyone from the car.

Her husband, J., was a very large and bearlike figure and at the time was working as a cement truck driver. They were enjoying life with a good income and all the benefits to match. So, when this accident occurred, thank goodness, they had excellent health benefits.

I was told the rescue was not easy, being up in the mountains. By the time the rescue team reached the accident site, they had to traverse the cliff to bring each one up separately. It took the longest to get A. out of the wreckage.

J. told me that in the beginning there was a lot of good care, insurance, and money. This happened about two years ago and soon every bit of the goods ran out. Money, insurance, and then even his job. He says he needed to stay home and take care of his wife and his kids. Now they basically had nothing and what family they had was back in Tennessee.

Going back to my first visit, a day I will never forget! It was late fall in California and was dark by 6:30. I came upon the property in an old section of Van Nuys and what looked like an abandoned house on a quarter acre of land. Driving up the dirt road I could see faintly all the windows were covered with old raggedy towels. The structure looked abandoned because no care had been given to the house or property for years. A large old woodshed was my impression. Walking up to the only door, I saw there was no door! A large dirty old piece of fabric was the entrance. The place was dimly lit, and I went deeper inside myself with a prayer of protection, not knowing what I was going to find.

I called out softly and announced myself and my name as the visiting nurse. A man yelled from the backroom to come on in. I walked in and I was so shocked. I had never seen such poverty in all my years working as a nurse. Things in disarray and minimal furniture. To the left of the living room space was another room with a blanket tacked up. A young woman, maybe about in her thirties, peeked through and said, "My mom and dad are over there," and pointed to my right.

I heard J. say come on in. Again, there was a towel hanging on the doorway as the door. I ducked under and was again beyond shocked as to what I saw! A. was in a hospital bed on her side, lying in a huge puddle of brownish green poop. J. had a white painter's bucket at the bedside and he was scooping up the diarrhea with his hands and splashing it into the bucket.

"STOP! I will help you with a much more organized way to do this and more sanitary."

He was not even wearing gloves (I am sure it was because of not having money). When visiting nurses are ordered by the doctor, we can bring many needed supplies.

This is how we met for the first time, and of course, I jumped right in after gathering all my needed gear, gloves, mask, etc. The new family I had inherited was going to need a lot of education along with supplies.

The strange encounter made us grow close and they really trusted me and were happy when I arrived for my visits two days a week for over a year. During that time, I learned more about the family and that a man had donated his property rent free when he had heard they had no place to live.

Even though I knew I was helping the best I could, there was this sense of dread and darkness as I drove up that driveway. Not just poverty and the situation, so I would always sit in my car for a few moments and take a deep breath and say a protective prayer before I could even attempt to face what was inside.

After seeing them for a few months, things were a little cleaner and the family seemed to be using the nutrition and hygiene tips given. There was somewhat a sense of organization.

Walking in on this Saturday visit after announcing myself, Jack told me A. was running a fever. I was concerned because she had an indwelling urinary catheter. This is often an easy area to get infected and can be life threatening.

He directed me into the room where his daughter was standing over her, chanting! I asked her what she was doing, and she said she was a witch, and was making it go away and her mother better. I looked at her. "She needs medicine, and she will be healed through prayer, good care, attention, and the needed medicine. I don't think your witchcraft is working! Now please leave."

She stared at me then left.

These visits went on for almost a year. Toward the end of the year, during which I had taught and educated them, I informed the family I would be turning the case over to another nurse. My husband and I were moving to Kansas City. Of course, they were disappointed on hearing this news. Next week would be my last visit.

When I arrived for my last visit, it was a lovely cool day, and the birds were chirping and a gentle breeze caressed my face as I exited my car. I had a good sense of a job done to the best of my ability considering the circumstances. The reality of their dire situation was not going away, but I had taught them so many simple things to help them in their daily lives.

I stepped into the living room after announcing myself. As I turned the corner, they were all lined up in the living room, holding a homemade sign saying, "WE LOVE YOU AND WILL MISS YOU."

This brought tears to my eyes, and I was in shock!

They had even gotten my patient out of bed and up in a wheelchair. They then presented me with a gift of a small stuffed animal. This was so humbling to me that they made such an effort, especially knowing how they did without.

Learning to move beyond myself and caring enough to have love and compassion again, I was able to do the best job I could, and the reward was beyond measure.

37

The Mysterious
LIVING NEXT TO DARKNESS

Starting my day out in Kansas City, I was in my office and the nursing staff was discussing the schedules for the nurses. Everyone was concerned about this one patient who was living in a very drug-infiltrated area. It was known to have a lot of drug dealers and especially bad because it was a meth area, and meth makes people crazy! The concerns were for nurses with young children.

We as nurses knew we put our lives on the line every day in the neighborhoods we went into because of the random shootings always going on. There were conversations that if you were in the area where this was going on, it was being in the wrong place at the wrong time. Rarely have nurses or medical people been shot or hurt, but there have been dangerous things that have happened to all of us. One instance was a nurse in L.A. who had gone knowingly into a gang area. Her car was surrounded in broad daylight, and she was robbed of all her medical gear, syringes, and bandages. After that instance we were no longer able to wear our blue uniforms that could be associated with any potential gang affiliation.

The conversation was going back and forth, and I felt the need to step in and volunteer to be the nurse to go and see the patient. It was morning and the safest time to go. Anytime later in the day was dangerous. We all knew to be out of the hood by five. That was when the drug deals took place and a lot more shootings.

When I first worked in these areas and was naive as to what was really going on, I had stopped at a Taco Bell for a drink. It was around four o' clock. While sitting there I noticed a hired security guard coming to work there. He came over to me and started to chat with me and asked questions as to why I was in the area. I told him I was working as a nurse and going to see my last patient.

"Lady, you don't want to be around here after five or six. This all becomes a war and killing zone!"

I was informed and did some research on my own that this zip code I was working had the highest number of killings in Kansas City, Missouri. So now I was much more aware of certain areas and made sure I said even more prayers and walked with more awareness and attention.

I was told my patient was a retired veteran from the war in Vietnam and headed out to see him. He had developed a heart condition and I was to check his vital signs.

Within blocks of driving into the neighborhood, you could feel and see the changes take place. Many of the houses were in very poor condition and windows covered or boarded up. This was a very old neighborhood and was once a very prosperous place. White flight took place years ago and this hood never got renewed. I have to say there were so many of these neighborhoods being renewed and rebuilt in Kansas City, Kansas, and KC, Missouri, but not this one.

Suddenly I was in another world! The air felt thicker and hotter, and for the morning I saw a lot of cars coming and going on the street. I found the right address and pulled up to the curb right in front, which I was happy about. I sat cautiously to catch my breath and to assess the area and to say my prayers.

I was sitting quietly in my car with my eyes closed and trying to connect to myself and my deeper attention. There seemed to be complete quietness so I slowly opened my eyes. To my shock there was a car touching my bumper and two men looking straight into my eyes. They had literally crawled up to my car and were trying to intimidate me. Our eyes met and they did not look like your friendly neighbors. I slowly looked down and reached for my notepad and started to pretend I was writing. The fear and heat inside of me was very intense. I started to talk to the Lord on a personal level and asked for strength and protection. After what seemed like a really long time but actually was probably only five minutes, I heard their car door open. Now I was really scared but decided to not look up no matter what. A few minutes went by, and I slowly looked up and they were gone. Thank the Lord!

Looking back up at the house that seemed so far away, I saw my patient peering through the curtain, looking absolutely scared himself.

So now I felt safer and thought I would make a run for the front door because he would see me and would let me in right away. I looked around my car and the neighborhood and began to open my door and guess what? There was this huge and I mean huge black Pitbull sitting right next to my car just waiting for me to get out. No barking. Nothing. Just staring straight into my eyes.

Now my nerves were really on edge. The patient was still peering out of the curtains, waiting to see what I was going to do. I closed the door right away and called my best friend and sister in faith, told her what was happening, and asked for prayers. We both started to pray, and I had my eyes closed. After we prayed, I slowly opened my eyes, and he was gone! Just gone!

Always remember, "When two or more come together in My Name." It really worked!

I cautiously got out of the car and grabbed my Mary Poppins bag with all my medical supplies. Attentive and aware, I walked briskly towards the house. It was a hot steamy day, but my breath felt warm and comforting as I walked towards the poor-looking beat-up home that had not had paint and care for a long time.

My patient waited until I was right at the door before he opened it. Now I was feeling much more confident and very connected with myself. I had just witnessed a miracle, really!

Stepping into his house, I was looking with new eyes. I first looked at him and J. had such kind eyes as he greeted me, still in his bath robe.

"You were lucky!" he said. "Those guys are crackheads, and they are mean and came to next door to get their fix. That is a crack house next door to me. I live with this fear everyone day of my life, worse than Vietnam."

He was very happy I was there and wanted to share with me some of his treasures and things that brought him joy. I always loved sharing with patients, looking at pictures or pieces of art and things that bring such simple joy. This was one of the most important parts of my

DAILY MIRACLES AND ENCOUNTERS

job, *sharing*! Making that connection and trust was so necessary because soon I would be asking very personal questions about his health and intimates, taking vital signs, etc.

"Come over here and look at my treasures." He guided me to an old antique glass cabinet filled with little miniature toys. All polished and precious! It really was the sweetest collection I had ever seen. There were four shelves full of cars, trains, and dolls, with some lovely pieces of sparkling colored glass that gently lay between them. Everything in perfect order. He shared his most private things and heart with me. But wait! When he observed I was enjoying myself, he said, "Wait, let me show you why I am not scared living here."

I was starting to get a little impatient. I had a certain timeline and needed to check his vital signs and ask my questions, but I said, "OK, but then we need to check you out."

He agreed. He grabbed my hand and took me through a curtain hanging as a door into his kitchen. I was not nervous or afraid of him, but I was aware and had my feet connected to the ground. Walking through the kitchen, to the left was another cloth hanging as a door.

"Come look." His face beamed with excitement. Now I was very cautious as he pulled the curtain back. It was pitch dark in there where his bed was!

I hesitated, then he picked up a flashlight and flashed it on the walls, panning slowly from left to right. Around his bed he had hung all the things that were meaningful to him. War paraphernalia, flags, etc.

I was getting a little nervous and feeling somewhat vulnerable.

Then he said, "This is what protects me!" Over his bed was a large picture of Christ. This was his protection, and his very private room, and he shared his most intimate Love with me!

After I checked him out and he shared some of his Vietnam stories, he, like a gentleman, walked me to the door, and neither of us were fearful or afraid. We had both been lifted in this dark place with the gift of brotherhood and sisterhood all while amid darkness and living next to darkness! All is well in the world, my friends.

38

Unnerving

SCARED TO DEATH

I had committed to working an extra Saturday to see a few patients in L.A. Seeing that I only had a few to see, I used my time to run some errands and do a little shopping beforehand.

I was feeling good and lighthearted as I approached the apartment house to see my first patient. I was told and read on my report that he was a fifty-year-old man who had just been diagnosed with multiple sclerosis. I first called him on the phone. He was pleasant and invited me to come over. His apartment was on the second floor, so I took the stairs and knocked on the door. He opened the door and was a nice looking Middle Eastern man with a lovely smile and friendly. I noticed he was using a walker and had severe lower extremity weakness. He directed me in but as I stepped into the living room, he was talking nicely but reached up and locked the door with two dead-bolt locks and the regular knob lock. I had never had someone do this before and the thought flashed through my mind why was he doing this? But I did not listen to myself because I saw he was very weak and maybe used to doing this out of fear.

I asked him to go and sit where he would be the most comfortable so I could check him and take his vital signs. He said he would be the most comfortable sitting on his bed in the bedroom. Again, I paused, but it was very common to see patients in their rooms and in their beds, so I agreed. I followed him into his room. He sat on the bed and then invited me to sit next to him.

We started to talk and I was doing the initial intake of a new patient and asking all kinds of mundane but necessary questions. I needed his insurance information and upon asking he became very agitated and then informed me he had no insurance at this time. I tried to explain to him that he would have to apply for Medicaid insurance in California. the more I talked the more agitated he became to the point I was becoming very guarded speaking to him. As his temper became more enraged, I said I would call my office for information about his insurance. He started yelling at me. I became frightened, got up, walked to the side of the bed, and told him I was sure all would be OK. I would call my office for the information.

I walk past this screaming man to the right of the bed to get to the phone. He turned and pounded his fists on the dresser and blocked me in the corner of the room where the phone was. I did not have my cell phone with me! While he was still sitting on the bed, he was pounding and screaming, pounding and screaming, coming closer and closer to me and demanding I put down the phone! He terrorized me.

"OK, OK, what do you want me to do?" Standing in the corner, I dropped the receiver and put both arms and hands out and begged him to stop. He did not! Now I thought to myself I know how real victims feel, *trapped*.

He was still coming closer to me inch by inch and wanted to hurt me. All of this happened very fast but to me it occurred in slow motion. Survival mode kicked in and I thought, *he has no lower body strength. I must try and escape before he hits me.* I quickly looked at him and my bag on the floor. *I must grab my bag on the floor before I escape.* Then suddenly with the grace of the Lord and my guardian angel, I went for it and with full body strength took both arms and hands and ran towards him and with all my might shoved him in the upper chest.

He went toppling over on the floor screaming and yelling, "You bitch. I am going to kill you once I get my hands on you."

I reached over and grabbed my bag and went running to the front door. Now I was up against two dead bolts and a lock on the handle. I was in pure terror because he was crawling on his hands and knees toward me.

Have you ever had a dream that someone is chasing you and you try to get away and can't? Well, here I was in the nightmare in terror! I was losing it now and kept trying to get locks open and kept relocking them because I was not thinking straight! Suddenly peace came to my mind and a little voice said, "Keep calm, you have time because he has to crawl." I took a breath and my mind returned and I was able to unlock all the locks. Once out the door, I ran like hell yelling for help! No one came, but the manager's office was at the end of the stairs, and they let me in. I told them what happened and I called my office and reported the incident.

So many lessons were learned that day, and my incident was discussed with all nurses after a meeting about the occurrence. Our office started self-defense classes now available to nurses and told us never allow patients to lock the door behind you.

This also was a huge lesson for me to be aware and alert to my environment, especially when someone is really suffering and you are having a great day. Life can change in a moment. I don't think I could have changed the situation except for not locking at the doors behind me and not going into his room. This man was really hurting and was wanting to hurt someone else because of his pain. Hurting people hurt people!

Strange Tales
SEX, ANYONE?

I received a call from my office that Social Services had taken a man off the streets because he had bad injuries and burns over his body and was being released from the hospital today. They needed a nurse to go admit him to home health services and make sure he was doing OK alone. This was the first time he'd had his own apartment in several years.

Arriving at the complex, which was very pleasant, I went to the second floor and knocked on the door. The man, in his mid-sixties, answered and was very pleased to see me and welcomed me in. The social workers had done a great job finding him a place to live and helping with most of his needs.

The studio apartment had a single twin bed but with no bedding and a small TV on the floor. He had to sit on the floor to watch TV. I introduced myself and explained I was there to take his vital signs and to check and change his burn dressings if needed.

He was now sitting on his twin bed, and he did not seem to want to discuss how he obtained all his injuries. He did tell me he was from Florida and was here homeless and searching for his son whom he had not been able to find yet.

As I was leaving, I had compassion come over me for this man and his situation. I wanted to do more, so I informed him I would be back to bring him something and check on him later that afternoon.

He was my last patient, so I went home and got some linens, a pillow, and towels for him and decided to stop at the fast-food place and get him some food.

Arriving back at the apartment, I told him I brought him a few things to eat and some sheets and a pillow for his bed. He was beyond elated and very thankful for my kindness.

We set all his food and drink on the floor, and he sat in front of the TV, eating his Big Mac and watching cartoons. I went over and made his bed. I felt very happy and fulfilled helping another human being, and he looked like a little child sitting on the floor watching cartoons.

It was as if there was a contentment we both felt in that moment. Just as I was thinking this, he turned to me and said, "Can we have sex now?"

I looked at him, laughing and said, "Big no."

"OK." He continued to watch TV. After all he was from the streets and what harm in asking!

The Mysterious
A SOUL CONNECTION

One of the patients I needed to visit during my break from regular adult nursing was a small child less than a year old who had been born with a terrible anomaly. The report I received was that he had a feeding tube and was barely responsive.

This case was during the time when I took the government contract for six months to have a break from all the endless paperwork associated with home adult care.

The report on the child and the family was that they were a very young couple, both his mother and father living in the home and both willing to take care of the child. In other words, they were loving and willing to provide for their sick child. This was really rare because I had seen over and over that when a child is sick long term, many times the men leave because they feel very frustrated not being able to fix the situation.

As I drove up to the house in the hills near the San Fernando Valley, I enjoyed the older neighborhood with many trees and early 1920s style cottage homes. I sat in my car and took a deep breath and said a meditative prayer to connect with myself and prepare to go into a not pleasant situation with a very sick child and young parents.

The house sat on a large hill, so I had to climb the stairs, carrying my nursing bag and a baby scale to weigh the child. Not an easy task but always doable with my Mary Poppins bag, that's what I called it!

At the top of the stairs was a pleasant small porch and while ringing the doorbell I again took a deep breath to the ground and center myself. A friendly young man with a warm smile answered the door. I guessed he was about twenty-two years old. He guided me into the living room and as I looked around, I saw a lovely little home with eclectic old furniture that was quite nice. I got a gut feeling of a caring home.

To my right was a small baby crib and the baby was there sleeping lying on his back. S. took me over to the crib and softly said, "This is my son whom I adore above all in the world!"

I looked up and saw tears in his eyes. He told me he accepted him and loved him just as he was. We both had a moment of being touched in the true language of love. This gave me the courage to do my job and filled me with compassion. I explained to S. I needed to take the baby's vital signs and to weigh him. He understood and agreed. Just then his wife came into the room. A tiny, less then one-hundred-pound woman looking frail and distraught and maybe around twenty-five years old. We were introduced and she agreed for me to check her baby's vital signs and agreed to help me to weigh him. The baby boy was smaller than most at his age, around one. I looked down with my heart aching and as gently as I could, checked him and looked at his G-Tube site. He was in a semiconscious state and only made sounds as I touched or moved him. He was a very perfect looking boy with soft white skin and pale-yellow hair covering his tiny head. His mother, J., helped me weigh him. While she was next to me, I could feel her pain and anguish.

After checking and finishing with the baby I asked J. and S. to please sit down. I had a few questions to ask about his medication and G-Tube feedings. We all sat and started to converse. I could tell they both felt comfortable with me and confident of my care. As we spoke, J. revealed to me she had not been feeling well and had lost a lot of weight. She suddenly said she had something to share with me. She wanted to show me something and left the room. She returned with a glass jar and in it was this huge knotted white mass! I tried not to look too shocked.

"This came out of my rectum this morning. What do you think it is?" She handed me the jar.

I felt shocked and could not believe my eyes. It appeared to be a huge, knotted tapeworm. I felt nauseated but at the same time was so pleased she felt safe enough with me to share and get my opinion. "I think it is a tapeworm but not knowing for sure, please follow up and take it to your doctor."

They both agreed. On top of all the care they had to do with their son, now this! Life sure can be tough at times along with all its beauty.

They were both so grateful for my visit and it was such a real genuine feeling among all of us. There was no denying it and we all shared this moment of love and caring together as human beings.

They escorted me to the door with a gracious "thank

you" as I left to go back to my car. Back in my car I sat for a moment to catch my breath and write a few notes. I took a deep breath and looked back up to the porch. S. was standing there just looking down at me with sadness and the kindest eyes. I looked up and our eyes met! We had a moment of real soul-to-soul connection.

I looked at him and nodded and then he to me.

The following week I was informed at my office that S. was killed in an automobile accident. I could not believe this added tragedy and sorrow to an already unbearable situation. But it was true, and he had moved on to another dimension however you believe or don't.

I had a chance to share one of his last moments on Earth. A very awakening soul-to-soul encounter I will never forget and feel so blessed to have had the opportunity of meeting him. It was almost as if he knew he would not see me again. Who knows, but we are talking about love much bigger than ourselves.

On a positive note, his best friend stepped up to the plate and moved into the house and took over the care of his son and wife. If that became more permanent later, I do not know, but it seemed to me quite miraculous!

41

Strange Tales, Big Miracles
SICK DOGGIE

I had a visit scheduled to see one of my elderly patients who had had stroke, living in the inner city. She was doing very well, and this was about my fourth visit to see her. A few weeks before she was feeling so good that she said she wanted to get a dog to keep her company. So, I set her up with another one of my patients who fostered dogs, and she was able to get an adorable Pomeranian about two or three years old. She fell in love with him and he with her. My next visit I expected to find a healing and loving environment as I went up to the door. Just shows you where too much thinking can get you!

Knocking on the door I saw her through a small window on the door. She was moving slowly to open it for me. I did not hear the dog bark. As soon as she opened the door, she exhorted to me, "My puppy is sick, and I do not know what is wrong."

Looking over on the couch I could see him very lethargic, and he barely lifted his head. I knew as a nurse I was there to see my patient, but puppy got priority!

She pleaded, "Please, please heal my puppy."

Oh dear! I knew this was an important part of her

healing so I said I would do my best. I went over and gently sat down next to Frito, talking quietly to him assessing him while stroking his fur.

I saw as I stroked him that he was very ill. I said an inward prayer and waited for inspiration of what to do. Then I found out and started to work. I got out a large syringe and gave him filtered water that S. had on hand.

Then I went to my car where I had an emergency supply of homeopathic medicine in my car that I used for myself if I was out and about and did not feel well. I knew I could try because I had used these remedies for animals before for immunity, and they worked great.

Coming back, I carefully placed it under his tongue and again said an inner prayer. That was the best I could do, I told S. She nodded and felt more at ease. I finished my visit with Sally and said I would see her in two days, and we agreed, hoping for the best. When I returned, Sally greeted me at the door and was smiling and Frito was barking at me!

I was so happy to see the joy back for both. I sat down to assess S. Frito sat across from us on the couch, staring but his tail wagging. He really was a one-woman dog, so he did not come near me. Then suddenly he jumped off the couch and came to me and up he came to me, looked into my eyes, then just laid his head on my lap! We were so shocked. S. said, "He never does that to anyone accept me."

I was able to walk out having the greatest sense of joy having not only helped my patient but also assisted in giving back her love and joy, Frito!

42

Strange Tales, Big Miracles
MY HINDU PATIENT

This story takes me back to L.A. during a time when I was working at a holistic clinic and alternative pharmacy.

I was hired to work upstairs and consult with patients and customers who came in to have acupuncture and get alternative vitamins.

One day the practitioner of acupuncture came into my office and asked for me to come assess his patient he had on the table. He felt something strange and wanted my opinion because I was a nurse. I agreed and walked back to the room with him. Lying on his table was a lovely woman around seventy years old and very thin and frail. He introduced me to his patient and asked if she would allow me to feel her abdomen. She agreed. I slowly lifted her shirt and the doctor pointed to his concern. I took a deep breath and grounded myself in a deep awareness, connecting to my breath and saying an inner prayer. I walked my fingers started softly across her abdomen and up under her ribs. My knowledge and skills as a nurse along with my instincts told me that what I was feeling was not normal or natural. Trying not to inject fear I told the patient and the doctor that I thought it was very important to go and see a medical doctor as soon as possible. They both stared at me and gently nodded in unison that they understood. I walked out of the room, having given them my best.

That whole incident occurred in early September, and I did not hear anything else about that patient. We were so busy at the clinic we just let it go. She was not my patient and only came in for acupuncture once a year.

Then around the first of November, the doctor called me and asked if I would go and do a home visit nearby. I agreed and arrived in a nice older neighborhood in Woodland Hills in front of a lovely little blue and white cottage with a picket fence covered with flowers.

I knocked at the door and a nice young man answered the door, introducing himself as her son. M. was on the couch, even more frail and gaunt looking. I sat to the side of her, and she was wonderful and so grateful for my visit. As we spoke and I assessed her situation, she informed me she had no health insurance and just wanted to pass on here in her home. I was really shocked to hear that. Her son informed me he lived in Oregon and needed to get back to work. I encouraged them both and gave them local resources that I knew about as a nurse. The son was so upset and left the house.

As M. and I were left alone, she shared her life story with me and said she had been a practicing Hindu for many years after meeting a lovely guru in Paris where she was working painting silk scarves.

We had a meaningful visit and then I told her I had to leave. Before I left, she grabbed my hand, and asked "Will you please say the Our Father prayer with me?"

I agreed and together we shared and held hands and said the Our Father together!

I did not hear anything from her or family for a while, but I knew her time was limited. Then on Thanksgiving morning around ten, I got a call from her son stating she was in bad condition, and he had never gotten her on hospice care. I had a rare day off nursing and the first Thanksgiving off in a very long time. Turkey was in the oven, but I agreed to try and help and would get back to him.

I was probably on the phone for several hours, but finally with all the red tape and speaking to the head nurse on call, they agreed to take her case at no cost to the patient and family. She had been accepted to be seen as an indigent person who was unable to pay.

I called her son and informed him and told him to give M. my love and blessings and that a hospice nurse would arrive that afternoon. The sense of calm and peace was amazing, and I felt a real sense of thanksgiving that day!

Within one week M. passed on with the help and support of hospice with comfort measures and calming medications. This was truly a gift given to me and M. with the help of Divine intervention.

43

Unnerving

GIVING AWAY HER HEART

Occasionally to make a little extra money, I would pick up a shift in another hospital as a temporary float nurse. It was a small hospital close to my neighborhood, and it made for a nice change of pace working a Saturday shift from 3–11 p.m.

Upon arriving I was told in the nursing office that I would be working in ICU. My one patient was a twenty-eight-year-old woman who had fallen off her horse and landed on her head on hard pavement. I took a deep breath as the supervisor explained the whole situation and what my duties would be. I was to stay in the room with her and give her a bath, change head bandages if needed, and give basic comfort measures even though the patient was in a coma and now considered brain dead. On my shift they would do one more EEG to check for brain activity and then wait for the family who were flying to California to be at her side. They would have to decide if they would have her disconnected from the respirator and allow her to pass. Oh my gosh! This was beyond tragic, and I was in the midst of the drama and heartache.

The other part of the story was she was an organ donor, and everyone was waiting to get the OK from the family so they could rush her into surgery and transport her heart to UCLA by helicopter.

Walking into her room, I could only hear the slow methodical sounds of the respirator. I slowly moved towards the bed and was shocked to see that her head, though bandaged, was so swollen it was the size of a basketball! Her black and blue eyes were closed, and the bandages covered her whole head down to her eyes and her jaw. Only slits were open for her eyes. My heart sank, but I spoke softly and introduced myself as her evening nurse, knowing that hearing is one of the last senses to leave a human being before expiring.

I gently checked all her IVs and tubes, her urinary catheter, and all the respirator settings. Then I explained to her I was going to sponge bathe her and would be very careful and not let her get a chill. Preparing for her bed bath, I would uncover only parts of her body, wash then dry and cover them back up right away. I started with her right side and upper body, then to her trunk, then to her groin and private area, always covering her back up with a warm bath blanket. As I moved down her body, I took deep breaths and grounded myself on the floor, being as present and respectful as possible. I would always say an internal quiet prayer and look to the Divine for inner strength to do my job!

Lifting the blanket and exposing her left groin area, I was stunned to see the most delicate lovely tiny red heart tattooed next to her privates and left groin. It was such a sweet impression in the moment of who this lovely girl was and a testimony to her spirit!

Here was this tiny tattoo of a heart and soon she would be giving her heart away to another life in such a profound way.

My heart raced and then as I finished her bath, a nurse stepped in and informed me the family—her sister and father—had arrived.

Oh Lord! I don't know if my heart can take this!

They arrived, standing at the door of her room. Her sanctuary, her temple. You could feel all this sacredness in the room. I allowed them into the room and very few words were exchanged. There was no need for words. Not only did they have to see their daughter and sister the way she looked, but the father was also going to have to make the decision to take her off the respirator after the next EEG. *Oh Lord! Give us strength!*

I walked down the hall to give them time alone and tears could be heard all the way down the hall. I moaned and sobbed, and whispers filled the room and hallway.

After about twenty minutes, the father came out looking very strong but hurting so deeply. He grabbed my hand and said, "We have to let her go."

I was speechless and nodded.

He went to see the doctor. They had decided if the EEG, which was the third one, was still flat then they could pull the plug on the respirator.

When the EEG showed no signs of life, then everyone went into action. I stayed close and helped when I could. An operating room was being prepared and a helicopter was arriving in a few minutes with the staff to take her heart to UCLA.

Then everything went so fast. She was rolled into the operating room, and the family and I paced up and down the hallway. Waiting, praying internally, and just trying to be present in the moment and riding all the emotions that were presenting. At moments if her father looked at me with such sadness, it was almost unbearable but at the same time it was comforting.

Suddenly we could hear the helicopter landing in the back parking lot and two men in green scrubs came rushing through the emergency back doors holding a large insulated container. They made their way into the operating room, and we watched in shock. In a very short time they reappeared, this time almost running down the hall, and pushed the emergency doors open. They slammed shut, and moments later, we heard the helicopter take off.

We stared at each other in disbelief, and I reached over and touched her father's shoulder, and then I walked away. It was as if a part of our hearts had been taken also, but there was also the sense of goodness of someone waiting to receive her beautiful heart.

44

A Miracle

Is Anyone Listening?

In 2019 on a Friday, I had been teaching a therapeutic exercise class and had finished around 2:30 p.m. I felt great, not an ache or pain in my body. The night before I had read an article about a good safe practice of taking niacin to flush your circulation and what a great health measure it was to try. I always read about ways to keep my health and use preventative measures so I thought I'd try that. I remembered having a bottle of niacin in my cabinet, so after class I went looking for it and found it. The date had expired but I thought oh that should be OK. Maybe not as potent, which was all right because I knew it came with a strong flushing feeling while dilating the blood vessels. Before my husband and I went to dinner I took one 500 mg capsule of niacin.

We left for dinner to an Asian dinner place close by and walked into the restaurant. My husband looked at the menu and then we usually discussed what we would have together. I sat across from him and suddenly noticed this mild flushed feeling starting in my arms and slowly going down to my fingers. This did not surprise me, and I was curious and interested in observing how this was manifesting itself. Then a sudden flush on my face and neck. The flushing was getting more and more intense, and I felt a little nauseated and a slight sensation in my kidneys like an aching feeling. It became more and more intense, and my husband kept reading. I hoped he would look up and see what was happening and if he would be alarmed because I was slowly getting more and more alarmed! I finally got his attention. "Tony, look at me and what do you see?"

"Well, your face is really red."

"I know, and I don't feel well at all." I told him what I had done. "I think I am having a bad allergic reaction to the niacin. I am going to the door and get some air. If I am not back in a few minutes, please call 911."

He seemed shocked and agreed. I slowly walked to the door. By now my vision were very blurry. I had to get to the bench in front and put my head down or lay down. I felt I was going to faint. A man out front looked me in the eyes then simply turned away. I could see he did not want to be involved. My breathing became shallower. I sat down and dropped my head down between my legs and took deep breaths, but I got worse. Time stood still. I hoped my husband came soon!

I lay on the bench, put my feet up, and closed my eyes. Everything spun around, and as a nurse, I knew my blood pressure had dropped. At times I opened my eyes because I felt as if I was dying. *So this must be like what it feels like to die!* My husband suddenly appeared and looked down at me in distress. "Call 911."

He was shocked. "Are you sure, Yvonne?"

I nodded and he ran back into the restaurant for his phone.

I could hardly keep my eyes open as I began to drift into a heavenly light weight sense but still in the body. Again, I thought that I might die and then suddenly, I cried out, "Lord, help me. I do not want to die." And in that very moment a beam of Light struck me on the top of my head and I immediately was able to sit up in astonishment! I was instantly better! Very wobbly but 99 percent healed in an instant.

I shuffled into the restaurant and sat across from my husband.

He looked up at me in astonishment. "Yvonne! I couldn't find my phone. Do I still need to call 911?"

"No, go ahead and order your food. I'm fine, and I was healed! Just a little wobbly. I'll eat only rice, thank you."

This is yet another story to confirm the ongoing loving presence of our loving Father and presence of the Divine when we seek and are open to that which is oh so much bigger than ourselves.

This experience has stayed with me, and I have not stopped sharing the excitement of the Good News!

About the Author

Yvonne's spiritual journey took her from Catholicism to evangelism to studying many religions through books and then to the writings and books of Armenian mystic George Ivanovich Gurdjieff. This brought her full circle back to the Eastern Orthodox Christian Church where she has been a member for over forty years.

After a career as a nurse for over forty years, Yvonne now teaches therapeutic yoga exercises for alignment and general health.

www.ingramcontent.com/pod-product-compliance
Lightning Source LLC
Chambersburg PA
CBHW060830050426
42453CB00008B/640